Dec 2017

To Kelly,
Because with food, we all become
family.

— Mercedes

THE HUNGRY FAMILY COOKBOOK

I PROVIDE HEALTHY
TIPS THROUGHOUT
THE BOOK.

I WROTE THE RECIPES.
TOGETHER, WE ARE
DYNAMITE!

BERIT   **KJARTAN**

KJARTAN SKJELDE

THE HUNGRY
FAMILY
COOKBOOK

BERIT NORDSTRAND

PHOTOGRAPHS BY ARNE BRU HAUG

weldon**owen**

NOW, LET'S COOK!

INTRODUCTION

KJARTAN SKJELDE

ALL PARENTS WANT THE BEST FOR THEIR CHILDREN. I FULLY BELIEVE AND AM CERTAIN THAT THE WONDERFUL AND VARIED MEALS WE GREW UP WITH GAVE US OUR RESISTANCE TO ILLNESS. I HAVE COME TO THIS CONCLUSION AFTER TWENTY YEARS AS A COOK AND THE FATHER OF A FAMILY.

It has been shown that you can come to the same conclusion from another perspective: the scientific. In working on this book, I've had firsthand insights into Berit Nordstrand's research-based tips about meals. Berit is a doctor, a mother of small children, and a food expert who has both taste and health as her overall goals.

What's it like to produce a family cookbook that takes into consideration modern research on nutrition, flavors, and health issues? I had already thought about this and had some experience at home. Berit Nordstrand added to it with her concepts and new research.

Together, we developed a wide choice of dishes that are healthy, tasty, and follow modern research and sustainability. This is a package deal for all you conscientious parents who also have concerns about the environment, sustainability, and the ability to find pure, natural foods for cooking. We begin with the new Nordic cooking at the grassroots level. We are the base team for the Nordic chefs who have awakened the food world to quality fresh, healthy, good-tasting, and traditional foods, such as hawthorn berries, cloudberries, lingonberries, rowan berries, moss, spruce shoots, wild meat, wild fish, fresh seafood, seaweed, and kelp. These local whole foods have been important food sources for us. The price-conscious Nordic cook has shown what kind of food bounty is available to us here at the top of the world. Our own best practitioners have gone down to the grassroots and worked together with all those who have tirelessly sought to save our traditions and our cultural heritage. Together, the top chefs and those who want to preserve culture have created a tasty, Nordic-exotic, sustainable-food universe that has captured the world's attention. Also included on our team are experts who are concerned with climate, the environment, sustainability, nutrition, and health.

The focus on local products is now the core concept of most Norwegian home cooks and restaurant chefs. I am an optimist about the future. Our own admirable raw materials now enjoy respect from both the youngest prospective cooks and the most experienced star chefs. They know that authentic flavor comes when one uses just-picked, newly harvested, just-fished or recently slaughtered local foods. You don't need to look far for something similar. Consciousness about meals has spread as much among consumers and producers as in restaurant kitchens. To live in step with nature's own principles is an old guide for life, but the method of doing this changes over time. You can experience my methods in practice by using the recipes in this book. My dishes originated from work experience, life experience, the positive influences of colleagues and experts, and my role as the father in a family with three children. I want us, as a family, to eat well while also considering both health and sustainability—that has been the guiding principle for my selection of recipes in this book.

GOOD FOOD

When I think back on it, our childhood meals were always delicious. The whole family gathered around the table. No matter what was on the menu, the food was homemade, tasty, and varied. In the days before Christmas, there was always anticipation in the family about Grandmother's Christmas dinner. Pork cutlets were not very traditional for Christmas dinner, but they always tasted fantastic because the meal united the entire large family in strong feelings of togetherness and tradition.

My normal and secure upbringing was filled with healthy, authentic, and homemade food. So it became natural for a guy like me, who liked activities better than schoolbooks, to choose a career where I could work with something I connected to. As a chef, I could change familiar basic ingredients into something tasty and delicious for sophisticated guests. Through this career choice, I could also gain entry into foreign cultures that I had only read about. All the expectations I had for work were soon fulfilled. I was able to seek out fantastic flavors, exciting combinations, and new processes together with like-minded colleagues. I traveled around and met professional cooks who had already reached the desired results in the search for good flavors. Through study periods and travels, I was also able to see that people in other cultures searched for local flavors among their own raw ingredients and their common knowledge.

Around the turn of the century, I was hired as the person responsible for food on the sailboat *Djuice Dragons* in the Volvo Ocean Race. I trawled the market squares and food markets in Africa and South America, among other places. An experience in Brazil in 2001 was an eye-opener. I stood under a mango tree for the first time. *Mango*—even the name is exotic, and the mild, tantalizing taste of a foreign

world. The juice running down my chin was a bonus. It was alluring to press gently on the red-green peel and get a light push back: *take me, I'm ripe.* I was finished thinking, desirous, with hands ready to pick my first mango fruit right from the tree. Perhaps it was exactly at that moment, when I took that first bite, that the concept of local food took hold of me. The mango that I had a taste picture of from Norway was completely different in its home in Brazil—the taste of this perfect, juicy, fresh, fruity mango was nothing like what I had experienced back home. For that reason, there aren't any mangoes in this book. However, there are time-honored versions of the basic foods that I grew up with: newly caught fish; shellfish; lamb in season, fresh meat with shiny, visible fat; just-picked fruit and berries; and newly harvested vegetables, grains, and dairy products that the food industry has not tampered with.

In just the twenty years that I have been a cook, the food world has changed drastically. When I started, all the exotic ingredients we could find in our Norwegian shops were especially tantalizing. In the last ten years, there has been exploitation of resources in the sea and on land. The food industry has changed for the worse, because consumers, in their eagerness for healthy food, and with the support of official experts, have been tempted to exchange flavorful foods for easy alternatives. Wild fish have been threatened both by overfishing and the practices of commercial fish farming.

WHAT IS GOOD FOOD THEN?

It was much easier to give a clear answer to this question in my childhood. The food that my parents chose for us children on the market square and at the butcher shop or in the grocery was tastier and healthier because, for the most part, it was locally produced by small-scale farmers. Today, when I'm searching for groceries for the family meals, I have to look through the food choices that the managers of a few grocery chains have decided should determine Norwegians' meals. We look in vain for cabbage just cut from a neighborhood field or fresh fish brought to the quay that morning. We have to pick through packages of meat to find a piece that has not been cut to conform with the recommendations of the authorities concerning "lean meat for the populace." I have, in common with many concerned Norwegians, found research that reveals the joke about fat: no one becomes slimmer by cutting out whole milk in daily meals. Only the food industry gains when the authorities drain away good flavor and nutritional value in meat and dairy products.

The "five-a-day" meal guides that we adhere to could really be six, but not five or six of just anything. If you buy imported fruit and vegetables, they are scarcely full value. Fruit from the other side of the globe, whether it's a mango or a banana, was picked before it was ripe. Imported vegetables might have been harvested too soon. This has quite an effect on flavor but can also have an effect on nutrition (completely ripe products offer a complete range of nutrition). Perhaps, though, an even larger threat to nutrition is the uncontrolled use of pesticide sprays. With produce such as broccoli and cauliflower, it is impossible to completely remove pesticide residue. In addition, the larger international commercial growers have developed plant species that grow more quickly. Unfortunately, harvesting too early and quick growth come at the expense of nutrition, according to recent studies.

MY DAILY PURCHASES

At the meeting point between flavor, nutrition, and sustainable production, I've gathered the ingredients for the recipes you'll find in this book. You don't need a special diet to live a long and healthy life. You do have to take care that you have balanced meals with all the building blocks needed for the body. You are invited to come along and choose a direction away from ready-made and industrially produced foods toward local and natural foods and dishes that you can make from scratch. Fortunately, many of us have grown up with these influences, and we want to spread them. These choices should also guide our purchases.

Grocery chains do not always play along with us. You can do something about that. As a consumer, you can demand that the selections on the store shelves be changed. So, the next round is up to you, to use natural foods that the stores supply.

You won't find refined white sugar in this book. Instead, I suggest honey. Farmed salmon is absent, but the book is full of excellent fish recipes. At the same time, Norway's traditional rich fish—herring—makes several appearances because herring doesn't just go into salads and snacks. I would tempt you to always have a jar of herring in the refrigerator, so you'll have one of the country's best and healthiest fast foods on hand. Organic eggs recur in the dishes, and you can find them in most local shops. You should also choose chickens that have had a good life, even if they are more expensive. If you are going to bake, choose organic spelt flour for a slightly higher price rather than ordinary flour. Both your taste and health deserve this. Choose tasty and authentic foods when you have the option.

THIS IS WHAT I BELIEVE IN

A lot has happened in the food world and society as a whole since I started cooking school in 1992. I am no longer quite so young but am just as curious. Flavor continues to be my overall goal. No matter how I accomplish the goal, it means more today than when I began my career.

I am now the father of three children, and that, of course, influences the way I think about food. In addition to flavor, health is at least as important. Healthy food is the precursor to healthy work. Food should be sustainable, enjoyed when it is fully ripe in taste and nutritional value, and it should have been raised naturally. I am so lucky to have vendors in my network who share my views on food. From them, I can find both great foods and inspiration. These guides include the enthusiastic Frode Ljosdal in the little village of Brimse. He is a pioneer who lives what he has learned from nature. As a rule, he offers new plants that he can recommend: vegetables, salad greens, herbs, and edible flowers. The key word is *seasonal*, which Frode emphasizes. Norwegians have a long way to go before we understand what's in our own best interest, which is to enjoy plants grown near us when they are completely ripe. Many believe that the Norwegian season lasts from June to September. However, in the mild climate of the outermost islands in the Bokna Fjord, the growing season can extend from May until the first frost in late autumn. Frode sows several times a year so he can harvest both early and on the far end of the season. With the help of strategic planning, he can have home-grown products pretty much year-round.

Once consumers realize that local food is important, they should also learn to vary their meals with new foods, says Frode. When root vegetables have finished for the winter, usually brussels sprouts, green cabbage, and kale are once again available. Luckily, the demand for kale has increased at the market over the past few years. In our district, one of the larger producers makes sure that the first kale is available in the produce section by May. Now people just have to learn how to use it all year-round.

Frode himself has a flavorful harvest in May, with home-grown lettuce, herbs, and sprouts, as well as ramps, baby carrots, baby turnips, tomatoes, cabbage, edible flowers, and later asparagus and summer vegetables. Every year, he broadens his assortment. Interactions between top local chefs and the rest of restaurants in Norway lead to new crops. He also keeps informed through the media. The surest way to control meals is to prepare dishes from the ground up and bake all the daily bread your family needs.

You can start by making healthy, tasty choices while you shop. You will also give your children a positive feeling and pleasure at the dinner table, something that is very important. In addition, you will be assuring that your local food traditions are passed on to the next generation.

I bake both bread and crispbread. Ancient grains such as spelt produce flavorful, nutrition-rich baked goods. Spelt flour is available at most shops, but for the largest selection of whole grains I shop at natural-food stores. By making food yourself, you can also control salt intake. Seventy percent of all the salt Norwegians consume annually comes from processed food. Salt, in and of itself, is not unhealthy, but excess consumption is not good; reasonable use of salt enhances the edibility of food and gives you beneficial minerals.

A MORTAR IN EVERY KITCHEN

Many modern cooks have counters and cupboards full of expensive cooking equipment. However, they don't seem to have room for the most sensible and wonderful work tool, the mortar. Do something about that. Go out and buy a mortar before you look through the recipes in this book. Crush whole spices so that flavor, aroma, and nutrients are available to you.

Need I say more …

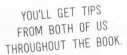

YOU'LL GET TIPS FROM BOTH OF US THROUGHOUT THE BOOK.

AND YOU'LL BE ALL THE HEALTHIER FOR IT.

A LOT HAS HAPPENED IN
THE FOOD WORLD AND
SOCIETY AS A WHOLE SINCE
I STARTED COOKING SCHOOL
IN 1992. I AM NO LONGER
QUITE SO YOUNG, BUT I AM
JUST AS CURIOUS. FLAVOR
CONTINUES TO BE MY OVERALL
GOAL. NO MATTER HOW
I ACCOMPLISH THE GOAL,
IT MEANS MORE TO ME
TODAY THAN WHEN
I BEGAN MY CAREER.

CHAPTER 1

BREAKFAST

YOU CAN ENJOY BREAKFAST OR CONSIDER IT AN EARLY DUTY. THE ONE THING YOU SHOULDN'T DO IS START THE DAY WITHOUT IT. THE FIRST MEAL OF THE DAY IS IMPORTANT. IT IS BY WAY OF THIS EDIBLE "FIRST CHAPTER," THAT YOU SET UP THE BUILDING BLOCKS FOR A GOOD DAY. FRESHLY MADE COFFEE, FRESHLY SQUEEZED JUICE, HOMEMADE JAM, NEWLY BAKED BREAD, SOFTENED BUTTER, AND A VARIETY OF TOPPINGS—FOR MANY PEOPLE, THIS IS JUST A DREAM OF HOW THEY WOULD START THE PERFECT DAY. HOWEVER, WITH SOME SIMPLE PLANNING, YOU CAN MAKE THIS DREAM BEGINNING OF A LEISURE DAY AN EVERYDAY EXPERIENCE: BAKE BREAD THE EVENING BEFORE, AND YOUR MORNING WILL START OFF WELL. MAKE MUESLI FOR THE WHOLE WEEK. PUT THE BUTTER AND JAM ON THE KITCHEN COUNTER SO THEY WILL BE AT ROOM TEMPERATURE WHEN YOU WAKE UP.

BREAD BAKED IN A DUTCH OVEN

No-knead bread can tolerate a long rising time. Prepare the dough
the evening before so you can shape and bake the bread the next day.
The result: freshly baked + homemade + real grain = fantastic bread.

MAKES ONE LARGE LOAF

1 package (¼ oz/7 g) active
   dry yeast (2¼ tsp)

2½ cups (625 ml) lukewarm water

2¾ cups (340 g) white spelt flour

4 cups (500 g) whole-grain
   spelt flour

1 cup (90 g) spelt flakes

3 tablespoons honey

1 teaspoon salt

2 tablespoons olive oil

In a small bowl, dissolve the yeast in the water. Set aside ¾ cup (90 g) of the white spelt flour for kneading. Mix the yeast with the rest of the ingredients by hand in a bowl, or in a stand mixer fitted with the dough hook. Work the dough for 1½ minutes. Cover the bowl with a damp kitchen towel and let the dough rise for at least 3 hours or preferably overnight on the kitchen counter. Scrape the dough out onto a well-floured work surface. Fold in the ¾ cup (90 g) reserved spelt flour with a spatula and knead the dough until it is elastic. Sprinkle the dough with flour and cover with a kitchen towel; let rise for 1 hour.

While the dough rises, position a rack in the center of the oven and preheat the oven to 475°F (250°C). Place the dutch oven in the oven at least 10 minutes before baking the bread to heat up the pan. Transfer the dough to the warm dutch oven. With the lid on, bake the bread for 35 minutes. Remove the lid and bake for another 15 minutes. Transfer to a wire rack to cool.

Why is breakfast important? During the night, the body rests and gets ready for a new day. So that the day will be the best possible, the first meal should consist of the best building blocks. Skipping breakfast usually leads to more snacking during the day and less nutrition, which in turn can lead to weight gain, Type 2 diabetes, weakened concentration and attention, and diminished vitality.

CRISPBREAD II

This crispbread is porous and full of flavor. Try this recipe with your own favorite seeds and grains.

1 cup (125 g) dark rye flour
¼ cup (60 g) rye kernels or dark rye flour
⅓ cup (30 g) rolled oats / ⅓ cup (90 ml) olive oil
¾ cup (90 g) pumpkin seeds
¼ cup (60 g) flaxseeds / ⅓ cup (45 g) sesame seeds
1⅔ cups (375 ml) water, preferably mineral water
Pinch of salt

Preheat the oven to 350°F (180°C). In a bowl, mix all the ingredients until the dough is moist but still lumpy. Spread onto two parchment-lined baking sheets. Bake for 15 minutes, then cut into squares. Return to the oven and bake for 45 minutes more. Transfer to a wire rack to cool.

CRISPBREAD I

This crispbread is rather dense, but the taste is unbelievable.

⅓ cup (45 g) whole-grain spelt flour
1¾ cups (220 g) white spelt flour
1 teaspoon fennel seeds
¾ cup (180 ml) whole milk / Pinch of salt

Position a rack in the center of the oven and preheat the oven to 350°F (180°C). In a bowl, mix all the ingredients until the dough is smooth. On a floured work surface, roll the dough out until thin and transfer to a parchment-lined baking sheet. Bake for 6–8 minutes. Remove the pan from the oven. Cut the bread into pieces with a knife. Return to the oven and bake for 4 minutes more. Transfer to a wire rack to cool. Store in an airtight container.

RED SMOOTHIES WITH OATMEAL

I've added rolled oats to this recipe so the smoothies will be complete meals on their own. If you want a thinner consistency, omit the oatmeal.

2 cups (250 g) frozen strawberries
1 cup (125 g) frozen blueberries
1¾ cups (430 ml) orange juice
¾ cup (180 ml) apple juice
3 tablespoons rolled oats / 1 tablespoon honey
1 banana, peeled and chopped / 1 handful ice cubes

Mix all the ingredients in a blender.

CLEMENTINE ORANGE DRINKS

I love all kinds of fresh-squeezed juice. If I had to pick my favorite, it would have to be clementine orange juice.

20 clementine oranges
¼ cup (60 ml) honey
2 handfuls ice cubes
Juice of 1 lemon

Squeeze the oranges; you should have at least 2 cups (500 ml) juice. Mix the juice and honey in a blender and then add the ice. Add lemon juice to taste.

MUESLI

Here's everything you need for breakfast—all on a tray. It's a giant portion
of muesli to make ahead for many breakfasts. Perhaps your neighbors or colleagues
would be happy to receive a jar of this fresh-toasted breakfast blend.

3 TABLESPOONS HONEY
1/3 CUP (90 ML) APPLE JUICE
1 TABLESPOON BUTTER
3 CUPS (270 G) ROLLED OATS
1 CUP (185 G) RAISINS
3/4 CUP (90 G) WALNUTS
1/2 CUP (60 G) FLAXSEEDS
3/4 CUP (90 G) SUNFLOWER SEEDS
3 1/2 OUNCES (100 G) SPELT FLAKES
OR ROLLED OATS
1/3 CUP (45 G) SESAME SEEDS
1/3 CUP (45 G) PUMPKIN SEEDS

Position a rack in the center of the oven and preheat the oven to 400°F (200°C).
Bring the honey and apple juice to a boil in a saucepan. Stir in the butter.
In a large bowl, mix all the dry ingredients with the honey mixture.
Spread the mixture on a rimmed baking sheet lined with parchment paper.
Bake for 15 minutes. Let cool completely before storing in an airtight container.

RED ENERGY DRINKS
4 SERVINGS

1 cup (430 ml) buttermilk
1¼ cups (155 g) raspberries
2 tablespoons honey
Blend until smooth.

DRIED FRUIT AND BERRIES

Choose freeze-dried berries, such as the strawberries and blueberries shown here, and serve with a sliced ripe banana and milk.

HONEY NUTS
¾ cup (90 g) hazelnuts
3 tablespoons honey

Toast the nuts in the oven. Rub with a towel to remove the skins. Mix the nuts with the honey.

WARM APPLE DRINKS

This drink is both spicy and strong.
If you like a little heat in your breakfast,
just add more chile.

2 CUPS (500 ML) APPLE JUICE
⅓ CUP (45 G) SLICED FRESH GINGER
¼ CUP (60 ML) HONEY
ZEST STRIPS OF 1 LEMON
6 SPRIGS FRESH CILANTRO
1 SMALL RED CHILE, SEEDED AND CHOPPED

Mix the apple juice and ginger in a saucepan and heat to 150°F (70°C).
Stir in the honey, lemon zest, cilantro, and chile.
Pour through a fine-mesh sieve. Serve warm.

In botanic terms, chiles are a fruit, but we use
them as a vegetable and a piquant spice.
Chiles are very versatile. If you want a rounder chile
flavor in your food, broil or roast the chile with
the skin on and then remove the burned skin.

To get the full effect of all the nutrition in this drink, with all the goodness of the greens, fruit, and honey preserved, don't make the drink overly hot.

WARM CARROT AND GINGER DRINKS

Healthy or sick with fever, sad or happy?
This drink will work for you no matter what your condition or mood.

3 POUNDS (1.5 KG) CARROTS
⅓ CUP (45 G) GRATED GINGER
2 CUPS (500 ML) ORANGE JUICE
2-3 TABLESPOONS HONEY
JUICE OF ½ ORGANIC LEMON

Juice the carrots and strain the juice into a container; you should
have 2 cups (500 ml) carrot juice. Mix the carrot juice with the ginger
and orange juice in a saucepan and carefully heat to 140°–150°F (60°–70°C).
Stir in the honey and add lemon juice to taste.
Pour the juice through a tea strainer or fine-mesh sieve to serve.

GREEN ENERGY DRINKS

This drink will kickstart your day. All the vegetables are pressed into juice.
Choose your favorite veggies and make your own energy drinks.

8 LARGE APPLES
1 MEDIUM BROCCOLI HEAD
4 OUNCES (125 G) SPINACH LEAVES
½ CUP (75 G) MINCED FRESH GINGER
2 TABLESPOONS HONEY
1 TABLESPOON APPLE CIDER VINEGAR
FRESH LEMON JUICE
ICE CUBES FOR SERVING

Cut the apples and broccoli head and stem into chunks.
Juice the apples and broccoli and pour half the juice into a blender.
Add half the spinach, ginger, and honey. Add 1½ teaspoons of the vinegar and
lemon juice to taste. Pour into a pitcher, and blend the remaining apple juice
mixture, spinach, ginger, honey, vinegar, and lemon juice.
Pour into the pitcher and serve over ice cubes.

Green vegetables such as broccoli and spinach contain a range of antioxidants that can suppress outbreaks of inflammation. They comfort you with fresh flavors, improve your immunity, and build strength.

RYE BREAD

Rye bread is excellent for flavor, a long shelf life, and nutrition.
This variation is lighter than traditional rye bread but is just as moist and good.

MAKES 2 SMALL LOAVES

1 package (¼ oz/7 g) active
   dry yeast (2¼ tsp)

3 cups (750 ml) lukewarm water

¾ cup (180 ml) buttermilk

3 tablespoons olive oil

4 cups (500 g) dark rye flour

2⅓ cups (295 g) light rye flour

1¾ cups (220 g) white spelt flour

⅔ cup (90 g) sunflower seeds

⅓ cup (45 g) flaxseeds

½ teaspoon salt

Dissolve the yeast in the water in a large bowl. Stir in the buttermilk and olive oil. Stir in the flours and seeds and mix until the dough is elastic. Add the salt. Cover the bowl with a damp kitchen towel and let rise for at least 1½ hours. Scrape the dough out on to a floured work surface; knead well. Divide the dough into two pieces and put each half into a buttered 4-cup (1-l) bread pan. Cover the pans with a kitchen towel and let rise for 1 hour.

While the dough rises, position a rack in the center of the oven and preheat the oven to 425°F (220°C). Bake the bread for 40 minutes. Remove the bread from the pan and check to make sure it is done: tap the bottom of the loaf; if it sounds hollow, then it is done. Transfer to a wire rack to cool.

This type of moist bread freezes well, so make a large amount to start with. The most practical way to freeze the bread is to slice it before freezing. Then, you just have to thaw the slices you want in the toaster.

MMM...

NUT SPREADS FOR THE WHOLE WEEK

When preparing food with nuts, make sure that the nuts are fresh (check the "best by" date, if available). The older the nuts, the more bitter they become. If you want to preserve most of the fatty acids in the nuts, reduce the oven temperature to 350°F (180°C).

NUT SPREAD

I grew up with peanut butter, and the flavor of roasted nuts and butter is a good memory. This spread gives me the same feeling.

1¼ CUPS (220 G) ALMONDS
1¾ CUPS (220 G) WALNUTS
⅓ CUP (80 ML) PICKLING BRINE
(4 PARTS WATER + 2 PARTS HEATED APPLE CIDER VINEGAR + 1 PART HONEY)
⅓ CUP (80 ML) OLIVE OIL
SALT

Preheat the oven to 325°F (160°C). Spread the almonds and walnuts on a rimmed baking sheet and toast in the oven for 10–15 minutes until fragrant and colored. Pulse the toasted nuts in a food processor with the brine and oil until the mixture has the consistency of nut butter. Add salt to taste.

NUGATTI SPREAD

Nugatti is a beloved Norwegian spread made with chocolate, hazelnuts, and nougat; it's similar to Nutella. Here's a more healthful version you can eat with a good conscience.

1¼ CUPS (220 G) ALMONDS
OR OTHER NUTS
⅓ CUP (80 ML) WATER
6 TABLESPOONS (90 G) BUTTER
⅓ CUP (80 ML) HONEY
3 OUNCES (105 G) DARK CHOCOLATE,
CHOPPED
1 TABLESPOON UNSWEETENED
COCOA POWDER
2 TABLESPOONS OLIVE OIL
SMALL PINCH OF SALT

Toast the almonds in a rimmed baking sheet in a preheated 350°F (180°C) oven for 6–8 minutes. Combine the water and butter in a saucepan and bring to a boil over medium-high heat, then add the honey. Pour the mixture into a food processor with the nuts and pulse until evenly ground. Add the chocolate to the blender with the cocoa, olive oil, and salt. Process until smooth.

MAYONNAISE

This mayonnaise is not only good on its own, it can also be used as a base for dressings or flavored mayonnaise.

1 EGG YOLK, AT ROOM TEMPERATURE
1 TABLESPOON MUSTARD
1 TABLESPOON APPLE CIDER VINEGAR
½ TEASPOON HONEY
⅔ CUP (160 ML) CANOLA OIL
⅔ CUP (160 ML) OLIVE OIL
JUICE OF 1 LEMON
SALT

Whisk the egg yolk, mustard, vinegar, and honey together in a bowl.
Drizzle in the oils, whisking until the mixture has thickened.
Add the lemon juice and salt to taste.

I can't repeat this often enough: homemade mayo is easy to make and tastes so much better than store-bought mayonnaise. The egg yolk thickens as the oil is whisked in. Make sure to whisk the oil in slowly so that the yolk binds well to the fat. All ingredients should be at room temperature before you begin.

You can enjoy fresh Norwegian shrimp with a good conscience. The shrimp are sustainable, the flavor is first class, and the quality is tops. Shrimp from the Norwegian fjords are especially good between November and February when the water is cold and brisk. In the States, look for Gulf shrimp.

SHRIMP SALAD

The amounts given here will provide enough for
one large breakfast group or several mornings.

1 EGG YOLK
1 TEASPOON DIJON MUSTARD
JUICE OF ½ LEMON
1¼ CUPS (310 ML) OLIVE OIL
3 TABLESPOONS SOUR CREAM
10 OUNCES (315 G) SHELLED SHRIMP
5 HARD-BOILED EGGS,
PEELED AND CHOPPED
2 SHALLOTS, CHOPPED
MINCED FRESH DILL
SALT AND CAYENNE PEPPER

Make a mayonnaise by whisking the egg yolk and mustard in a bowl
with the lemon juice and olive oil. Stir in the sour cream. Fold in the shrimp,
chopped eggs, and shallots. Season with dill, salt, and cayenne pepper to taste.

LIVER PASTE

Homemade liver paste, or pâté, is in a class by itself!
This makes a large amount, so you can freeze part of it before you bake it.
That way you can have freshly made liver paste for breakfast on several mornings.
Don't forget to reduce the cooking time if you decide to cook this in several small portions.

2 apples, peeled, cored, and diced

2 onions, finely chopped

1 garlic clove

5 sprigs fresh thyme

1 tablespoon butter

5 anchovies

2 eggs

1 teaspoon fennel seeds, crushed

18 ounces (190 g) pork liver, chopped

3 slices bacon, chopped

7 ounces (220 g) fresh pork fat (fatback), chopped

¼ cup (60 g) butter

⅓ cup (45 g) white spelt flour

1¾ cups (430 ml) whole milk

Preheat the oven to 350°F (180°C).

Fry the apples, onions, garlic, and thyme in the butter in a frying pan over medium heat until all the ingredients have softened and turned golden, about 10 minutes. In a food processor, process with the anchovies, eggs, and fennel seeds until smooth. Add the liver, bacon, and pork fat and process until fine. Make a white sauce with the butter, flour, and milk. Mix the sauce with the liver mixture and press through a sieve with the back of a large spoon.

Butter a baking dish that is the right size to contain the amount of liver paste you want to bake in a 1½-inch-deep layer. Pour the mixture into the buttered pan and bake for 40–45 minutes.

I often add anchovies to enhance flavor. They have strong aromatic flavor and can substitute for salt in some recipes. You can use them in salads, mayonnaise, purées, and sauces, as well as with meat and fish. Anchovies contain important omega-3 fatty acids and calcium.

SCRAMBLED EGGS WITH COTTAGE CHEESE

There's nothing as comforting as freshly made scrambled eggs to start the day.
Of course, you can have scrambled eggs for lunch, supper, or dinner as well.
No matter what time they're served, they should be eaten as soon as they are cooked.

1 tablespoon butter

8 eggs, beaten

2 tablespoons sour cream

1 tablespoon heavy cream

Salt and freshly ground pepper

Cottage cheese

Chopped fresh chives

Melt the butter in the top of a double boiler. Whisk in the eggs.
Stir in the sour cream and heavy cream. Season with salt and pepper.
When the mixture has thickened, transfer to a platter. Dot with cottage
cheese. Grind more pepper on top and strew with chives.

A double boiler, or bain-marie, is placing a bowl
(the double-boiler top) over a saucepan (the double-
boiler bottom) containing simmering water
to give you more control over the heat when working
with ingredients that shouldn't boil, such as egg
dishes or béarnaise and hollandaise sauces.

UNCOOKED BERRY JAM:
THREE VARIATIONS

Whichever variation you choose, it should be determined by the season.
When plums are in season, they should be added to the mix.

BLUEBERRY JAM
5 cups (625 g) blueberries

⅓ cup (80 ml) honey

2 tablespoons grated ginger

Grated zest and juice of ½ organic lemon

STRAWBERRY JAM
5 cups (625 g) strawberries

¼ cup (60 ml) honey

Juice of ½ organic lemon

½ teaspoon ground star anise

RASPBERRY AND PLUM JAM
1¼ cups (155 g) raspberries

12 (375 g) plums, skins removed and pitted

3 tablespoons honey

Juice of 1 organic lemon

Combine all the ingredients in a food processor
and pulse on medium speed to a smooth consistency.

There are so many different jams on the store
shelves. Most of them have a high percentage
of processed sugar. Making jam at home is an
easy and quick process. That way, you can be
completely sure of what is in the jam. You can
also make larger portions and freeze some.

CHAPTER 2

EVERYDAY MEALS

DINNER IS THE MOST IMPORTANT MEAL OF THE DAY, SO THIS IS THE
BIGGEST CHAPTER IN THE BOOK. IN MOST FAMILIES WITH CHILDREN,
THE EVENING MEAL IS THE ONLY TIME EVERYONE GATHERS IN THE
SAME PLACE. THE GROUPING AROUND THE TABLE PROVIDES
QUALITY TIME WHERE EVERYONE, BIG AND SMALL, CAN INTERACT.
"WHAT'S FOR DINNER?" IS THE QUESTION MANY CHILDREN ASK,
GREATLY ANTICIPATING THE MAIN MEAL OF THE DAY,
EVEN BEFORE THEY LEAVE FOR SCHOOL. DURING THE DAY, THEY
MIGHT SALIVATE AS THEY HAPPILY THINK ABOUT EATING
A CASSEROLE, SOUP, STEW, OR ONE OF THE OTHER TEMPTING DISHES
IN THIS CHAPTER. USE THE BOOK TO PLAN YOUR DINNERS
SO THAT YOU CAN DO THE SHOPPING ONLY ONCE A WEEK, WHICH
HELPS ENSURE VARIETY, EFFICIENCY, AND BUDGET MANAGEMENT.

CHEESY CAULIFLOWER WITH SMOKED HAM AND SALAD

This dish is tasty, healthful, and packed with all the flavor of a classic cauliflower gratin.
If you leave out the smoked ham, substitute with a vegetable dish.

SALAD

4 ounces (125 g) smoked ham

¾ cup (155 g) dried white beans, soaked overnight and drained

12 ounces (375 g) green beans, trimmed

2 hearts of romaine lettuce, chopped

¼ cup (60 ml) olive oil

Fresh organic lemon juice

Salt and freshly ground pepper

CHEESE SAUCE

3 tablespoons butter

3 tablespoons white spelt flour

2 cups (500 ml) whole milk

1 cup (125 g) grated Parmesan cheese

Chopped fresh parsley

Salt and cayenne pepper

4 small or 2 large cauliflowers, trimmed

LEFTOVERS?
DIVIDE THE CAULIFLOWER INTO FLORETS AND SERVE WITH A GREEN SALAD FOR LUNCH.

Preheat the oven to 400°F (200°C).

SALAD
Spread the smoked ham on a baking sheet lined with parchment paper and bake in the oven until golden and crisp, 5–10 minutes. Transfer to paper towels to drain. Cook the dried beans in a saucepan of salted simmering water to cover by 2 inches (5 cm) for 30–40 minutes, or until tender; drain. Cook the green beans in a saucepan of lightly salted boiling water for 3–4 minutes, or until crisp-tender. Drain. (You could steam the green beans in a steamer basket instead, if you like.) Combine the romaine hearts, drained beans, and crisp smoked ham in a bowl. Toss with the olive oil and then with lemon juice, salt, and pepper to taste.

CHEESE SAUCE
Melt the butter in a saucepan, whisk in the flour, and stir in the milk. Bring to a boil, then simmer for 10 minutes. Stir in the Parmesan and parsley, then salt and cayenne pepper to taste.

Preheat the oven to 325°F (170°C).

Bring a large saucepan of salted water to a boil. Add the cauliflowers, cover, and cook for 15–20 minutes, or until just tender; drain. Transfer the cauliflowers to a baking dish and pour the cheese sauce over them. Bake for 8–10 minutes, making sure that the sauce does not overflow and burn.

Divide the cauliflowers among 4 plates, cutting the cauliflowers in half if needed, and spoon the salad around them to serve.

When buying vegetables, it's always best to choose organic if you have the option. They will cost a bit more, but they're worth it.

SUNCHOKE SOUP WITH GOAT CHEESE AND CROUTONS

This soup is vegetarian. The onions and sunchokes add so much flavor
that they don't need any help from chicken broth.

SOUP

3 tablespoons canola oil

6 onions, finely chopped

1 pound (500 g) unpeeled
  sunchokes (Jerusalem
  artichokes), finely chopped

2 tablespoons minced fresh thyme

3 bay leaves

2½ cups (625 ml) water

Salt and freshly ground pepper

¼ cup (60 ml) olive oil

PICKLED ONIONS

¾ cup (180 ml) water

⅓ cup (80 ml) apple cider vinegar

⅓ cup (80 ml) honey

8–12 small onions

CROUTONS

6 slices bread, preferably
  white spelt bread

½ cup (60 g) hazelnuts,
  toasted and skinned

2 tablespoons olive oil

Salt and freshly ground pepper

5 ounces (170 g) fresh white
  goat cheese

Watercress leaves

SOUP

Heat the oil in a large pot and brown the onions and sunchokes with
the thyme. Add the bay leaves and then the water. Cover and simmer the
mixture for 40 minutes. Season to taste with salt and pepper. Stir in
the olive oil.

PICKLED ONIONS

In a saucepan, bring the water and vinegar to a rapid simmer, stir in the
honey, and let cool. Divide any larger onions into smaller pieces. Simmer
the onions in lightly salted water until tender. Add the cooked onions to
the vinegar mixture, and let cool to room temperature, about 20 minutes.

CROUTONS

Preheat the oven to 400°F (200°C).

Cut the bread into rough squares. Coarsely chop the nuts. Toss the bread
and nuts with the olive oil and season with salt and pepper. Transfer the
mixture to a baking pan lined with parchment paper. Bake until golden,
10–15 minutes.

Serve the soup in deep bowls and top with the croutons and nuts.
Crumble the goat cheese over the soup. Sprinkle on the watercress and
garnish with pickled onions.

LEFTOVERS?

THIS SOUP IS ALMOST BETTER THE NEXT DAY. IT ALSO MAKES AN ESPECIALLY GOOD BASE
FOR SAUCES AND OTHER SOUPS.

Pickled onions appear weekly in my refrigerator.
I always make a large amount of them,
as sweet-and-sour onions go with most dishes
as a side or as a recipe ingredient. Why not give
your host a pretty jar of pickled red onions
the next time you are invited out?

Vegetables are an important source
of nutrition for a good and healthy life.
They add lightness and freshness
to our meals and are ever so tasty.

ROASTED ROOT VEGETABLES WITH YOGURT DIP AND GOAT CHEESE

This is a vegetarian dish that can easily be supplemented with fish or meat, if you like. When it comes to fresh goat cheese, choose a tangy firm white goat cheese rather than a creamy one.

HERB BUTTER

½ cup (125 g) butter, at room temperature

2 garlic cloves, minced

2 tablespoons minced fresh tarragon

Salt and cayenne pepper

Juice of ½ organic lemon

2 parsnips

4 parsley roots

1 small rutabaga

4 red beets

2 yellow beets or turnips

2 red onions

2 yellow onions

7 ounces (220 g) fresh white goat cheese (1 firm round)

YOGURT DIP

⅓ cup (80 ml) plain Greek yogurt

2 tablespoons minced fresh parsley

2 garlic cloves, minced

Salt and cayenne pepper

Fresh organic lemon juice

Watercress leaves, for garnish

HERB BUTTER

In a bowl, beat the butter with the garlic. Stir in the tarragon and season to taste with salt, cayenne pepper, and lemon juice.

Preheat the oven to 400°F (200°C).

Trim and peel the vegetables and cut them into large pieces, except cut the onions in half crosswise. Put the vegetables into a roasting pan and stir in the herb butter. Roast until all the vegetables are tender, 30–40 minutes. Turn the vegetables a couple of times as they roast. In a dry frying pan over medium heat on the stove top, toast the goat cheese until golden, 1–2 minutes on each side. Cut into wedges to serve.

YOGURT DIP

Put the yogurt in a bowl and stir in the parsley and garlic. Season to taste with salt, cayenne pepper, and lemon juice.

Serve the roasted vegetables and toasted cheese garnished with watercress leaves, if using, and with the yogurt dip alongside.

LEFTOVERS?

REHEAT THE VEGETABLES THE NEXT DAY AND SERVE THEM WITH A PIECE OF FISH OR MEAT.

CABBAGE AND LEEK SOUP

Pointed cabbage doesn't just have a distinctive shape, it is also much sought after, with a more delicate flavor than other members of the cabbage family. Previously, pointed cabbage was a seasonal phenomenon in Norway and only in the stores in early summer. Now you can find it most times of the year. In the United States, it's available in farmers' markets and is also called sweetheart cabbage; napa cabbage is a good substitute.

SOUP

1 pointed (sweetheart) or napa cabbage, cored

1 leek, white part only, sliced and rinsed

2 shallots, or ½ yellow onion

3 tablespoons butter

¾ cup (180 ml) whole milk

⅓ cup (80 ml) plain Greek yogurt

1 bay leaf

Salt and freshly ground pepper

Fresh organic lemon juice

SALAD

½ cup (90 g) pearl barley, soaked overnight

Salt and freshly ground pepper

2 leeks, white part only, sliced and rinsed

¼ cup (60 ml) olive oil

Juice of 1 organic lemon

4 slices cured ham

½ pointed or napa cabbage

Watercress sprigs or pea shoots

LEFTOVERS?

THIS SOUP IS ALSO GOOD COLD. ADD A COUPLE TABLESPOONS OF SOUR CREAM AND SERVE WITH BREAD FOR LUNCH.

SOUP

Finely chop the cabbage, leek, and shallots. In a soup pot, melt the butter and sauté the vegetables for 3–4 minutes. Add the milk and then stir in the yogurt. Add water to cover. Add the bay leaf. Bring to a boil, reduce heat to a simmer, cover, and cook for 30 minutes. Season to taste with salt, pepper, and lemon juice. Remove the bay leaf. Purée the soup in a blender or food processor until smooth. Serve as is for a thicker, more nutritional soup, or strain the soup through a sieve.

In a saucepan, simmer the barley in salted water for 30–40 minutes until tender; drain. While the barley cooks, preheat the oven to 400°F (200°C). Put the leeks in a baking dish and season with salt and pepper. Pour over the olive oil and drizzle with lemon juice. Cover with aluminum foil. Bake the leeks until tender, 20–25 minutes. Spread the ham slices on a baking sheet lined with parchment paper. Bake until crisp during the last 5–10 minutes of the leek baking time. Chop the cabbage into thin strips and toast in a dry frying pan. In a bowl, combine the leeks, cabbage, barley, and crisp ham. Divide the mixture among warm soup bowls. Pour in the soup and garnish with watercress.

Don't forget that we also eat with our eyes. The presentation of food affects how it tastes. It doesn't take a lot to make the food more enticing—for example a simple garnish of fresh herbs is always attractive. A colorful or interesting table setting also makes food more inviting.

FARMER'S OMELET

One of the first meals I made by myself as a child was a farmer's omelet.
It is so easy to prepare that anyone can do it successfully.
If possible, use organic eggs. Serve the omelet with a fresh, green salad.
Pickled beets and toasted rye bread with a coarse mustard are tasty accompaniments.

½ cup (90 g) pearl barley,
   soaked overnight

Salt and freshly ground pepper

1 small head of broccoli

2 onions, coarsely chopped

3 tablespoons canola oil

2 cups (6 g) lightly packed
   baby spinach

6 eggs

¾ cup (180 ml) whole milk

10 ounces (310 g) smoked trout

1 bunch garden cress or
   watercress

In a saucepan, cook the barley in lightly salted simmering water to cover until tender, 30–40 minutes; drain.

Preheat the oven to 350°F (180°C).

Blanch the broccoli in a saucepan of lightly salted water for 2 minutes (or steam in a steamer). In a frying pan, sauté the onions in the olive oil until translucent. Add the spinach and broccoli. Set the pan aside. Whisk the eggs and milk in a bowl and season with salt and pepper. Pour the mixture into a baking dish. Add the cooked barley and smoked trout. Bake until cooked through and firm, 15–18 minutes. Garnish with garden cress sprigs and serve.

LEFTOVERS?

SLICE THE COLD OMELET AND SERVE IT ON
BREAD THE NEXT DAY, PREFERABLY WITH A
GREEN SALAD. IT MAKES A GREAT LUNCH!

Chickens that live and eat naturally lay eggs
that are more flavorful. Unfortunately, eggs were on
the dietary "blacklist" for some time. Now they are once
again considered healthful, and most people can eat
one a day with a clear conscience.

CELERY ROOT SOUP WITH HERBED TOASTS

This dinner dish offers multiple options. You can enjoy it as is, with bacon, or substitute croutons for a great vegetarian dish.

SOUP

2 celery roots

Butter, at room temperature

⅓ cup (90 g) rock salt for baking

1¼ cups (310 ml) whole milk

1¾ cups (430 ml) heavy cream

¾ cup (180 ml) plain Greek yogurt

⅓ cup (80 ml) water

Salt and cayenne pepper

Fresh organic lemon juice

5 slices thick-cut bacon or fatback, cut into squares (optional)

4 slices bread, preferably white spelt

HERB OIL

Leaves from 6 fresh parsley sprigs

⅓ cup (80 ml) olive oil

1 garlic clove

Grated zest of ½ organic lemon

1 tablespoon fresh organic lemon juice

Butter, at room temperature

Watercress, chervil, or parsley sprigs

Preheat the oven to 350°F (180°C).

SOUP

Wash the celery roots and cut them in half crosswise. With a sharp knife, cut an outline inside the rim so you can make "bowls" after the celery root is cooked. Generously butter the cut surfaces.

Spread the rock salt in the bottom of a rimmed baking pan. Put the halved celery roots in the pan with the cut edges up. Cover the pan with aluminum foil. Bake for 45–50 minutes until tender. Transfer from the oven and use a large spoon to scoop out the inside of the celery roots. Pulse the celery root flesh in a blender or food processor with the milk, cream, yogurt, and water. Using the back of a large spoon, press the mixture through a sieve into a saucepan. (You can omit straining the soup to preserve all the nutrients, but the soup will be thicker.) Heat the soup and season to taste with salt, cayenne pepper, and lemon juice.

In a dry frying pan, fry the bacon, if using, until crisp. Toast the bread in a toaster.

HERB OIL

Mix all the ingredients and pulse in a blender.

Butter the toasted bread and top with the watercress sprigs. Pour the soup into the celery root shells. Drizzle the herb oil on top and sprinkle on the crisp bacon, if using.

LEFTOVERS?

THIS CELERY ROOT SOUP TASTES GREAT COLD.

Refined all-purpose wheat flour has good baking qualities but does not have all the nutrients the body needs. Substitute whole-grain spelt or whole-wheat flour for more nutrition and less starch and gluten. You can also try some of wheat's ancestors such as the ancient grain einkorn.

FROM

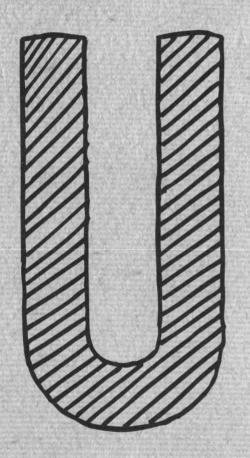

TO YUM

PICKLED TROUT WITH SALAD AND POTATO PANCAKES

Trout, potatoes, and boiled eggs—doesn't it sound more like weekday rather than party food? Everyone who leaves the table after this delicious and comforting meal will remember it as a tasty feast and will want a copy of the recipe.

4 trout fillets (1¼ lb/625 g total)

Salt

⅓ cup (80 ml) apple cider vinegar

⅔ cup (160 ml) water

2 bay leaves

1 teaspoon black peppercorns

¼ cup (60 ml) honey

4 eggs

POTATO PANCAKES (MAKES 4)

10 ounces (315 g) fingerling potatoes

3 tablespoons white spelt flour

1–2 whole eggs

2 tablespoons sour cream

1 teaspoon canola oil

Salt and freshly ground pepper

1–2 egg whites

Canola oil

SALAD

1 red onion

2 green onions

2 cups lightly packed baby lettuce leaves (60 g)

Fresh dill sprigs

Minced fresh chives

¼ cup (75 g) trout or salmon roe

¼ cup (60 g) sour cream

Sprinkle the trout fillets with salt and place in a nonreactive frying pan.

Mix the vinegar, water, and spices in a nonreactive saucepan and bring to a boil. Remove from the heat and add the honey. Fifteen minutes before serving, pour the warm brine over the trout and set aside.

Boil the eggs for 6 minutes. Rinse under cold running water, then peel and cut each in half crosswise. Set aside.

POTATO PANCAKES

Boil the potatoes in a saucepan of lightly salted water until tender; drain. Process the potatoes in a food processor with the flour, whole eggs, sour cream, and oil. Season with salt and pepper. Whisk the egg whites in a deep bowl until soft peaks form and fold into the potato mixture. In a frying pan, fry four pancakes in oil until crispy; keep warm until serving time.

SALAD

Cut the red onion into thin slivers. Chop the green onions. In a bowl, toss the onions with the lettuce, dill, and chives.

Place a fish fillet on each potato pancake and arrange the hard-cooked eggs, trout roe, and salad on and around the trout; dollop with the sour cream.

LEFTOVERS?

MAKE A FISH PASTE BY BLENDING THE FISH WITH SOUR CREAM IN A FOOD PROCESSOR. SPREAD THE PASTE ON BREAD OR ANY LEFTOVER PANCAKES.

Organically farmed fish such as trout or salmon are produced under strict environmental regulations. This method of production has a smaller impact on nature than regular fish farming. At the same time, a great deal of consideration is given to the welfare of the fish. Organically raised fish eat only natural fish food from sustainable sources, and the operation has strict routines to prevent the fish escaping.

OVEN-BAKED COD WITH TOMATOES AND POTATOES

I like to prepare food in a baking dish. The oven does all the work,
and the dish can also be used for serving.

1½ pounds (750 g) unpeeled
fingerling potatoes, sliced

3 onions, sliced

8 upeeled garlic cloves

4 cups (750 g) cherry tomatoes

5 ounces (155 g) roasted peppers
(from a jar), coarsely chopped

1 cup (125 g) black olives, pitted

3 bay leaves

½ cup (125 ml) olive oil

¾ cup (180 ml) water

1¼ pounds (625 g) cod, halibut, or
other white-fleshed fish fillets

Salt and freshly ground pepper

Fresh organic lemon juice

Coarsely chopped fresh parsley

AÏOLI

1 egg yolk

1 tablespoon apple cider vinegar

1 tablespoon mustard

1¼ cups (310 ml) olive oil

Salt and cayenne pepper

Fresh organic lemon juice

2 garlic cloves, minced

Toasted bread for serving

Preheat the oven to 350°F (180°C).

In a baking dish, combine the potatoes, onions, garlic, tomatoes, peppers, and olives. Add the bay leaves. Add the oil and then pour in the water. Bake in the oven for 20 minutes. Cut the fish into squares and season to taste with salt, pepper, and a few drops of lemon juice. Place the fish pieces on top of the vegetables in the pan. Bake for another 7–8 minutes, or until the fish is cooked through. Sprinkle with parsley.

AÏOLI

In a bowl, whisk the egg yolk with the vinegar and mustard. Whisk as you add the oil in a thin drizzle until the aïoli is airy and completely blended. Season to taste with salt, cayenne pepper, and a few drops of lemon juice. Fold in the garlic.

Serve the fish and vegetables with the aïoli and toasted bread.

LEFTOVERS?

THIS DISH CAN EASILY BE REHEATED THE NEXT DAY. COVER THE BAKING DISH WITH A LID OR ALUMINIUM FOIL AND HEAT GENTLY.

We know that the omega-3 fatty acids in fish fat is healthy, but did you know that lean fish also gives you iodine for your metabolism? Some studies show that cod has the kind of protein that can make it easier for you to control your weight.

GRILLED MACKEREL AND LENTIL SALAD

This combination is one of the best I know of, and it's a tasty summer classic in my family. Mackerel with cream is one of my favorite childhood memories.

Salt and freshly ground pepper

⅓ cup (45 g) white spelt flour

8 mackerel fillets, skin on

¼ cup (60 ml) canola oil

⅔ cup (160 g) crème fraîche

Fresh organic lemon juice

Minced fresh parsley and chives

LENTIL SALAD

3½ oz (105 g) French green lentils

1¼ cups (7 ounces) shelled green peas

2 cups (250 g) sugar snap peas

2 tablespoons olive oil

5 slices bacon, chopped

1 heart of romaine lettuce, chopped

Salt and freshly ground pepper

LEFTOVERS?

MASH THE REMAINING MACKEREL WITH CRÈME FRAÎCHE AND USE IT AS A DIP FOR FRESH VEGETABLES.

Mix the salt and pepper with the flour in a resealable plastic bag; shake the fish in the bag to coat it with the mixture. Brush off the excess flour. Heat the canola oil in a frying pan and fry the mackerel, skin side down, until the skin is crisp and golden. Sprinkle with salt. Transfer the fish to a serving dish. Add the crème fraîche to the pan and season to taste with salt, pepper, and lemon juice. Add the herbs to the sauce and bring the sauce to a simmer. Set aside and keep warm.

LENTIL SALAD

Simmer the lentils in a saucepan of lightly salted water to cover until tender, about 20 minutes. Cook the peas and sugar snap peas in a saucepan of lightly salted water until tender. (You can also steam the vegetables over salted water in a steamer to help preserve more of the nutrients.) Heat the olive oil in a frying pan, add the bacon, and fry the bacon until crisp; using a slotted spoon, transfer to paper towels to drain. Toss the lettuce with the lentils, vegetables, and bacon. Season to taste with salt and pepper.

Serve the fish with the salad and cream sauce.

Regular sour cream can separate when heated, but crème fraîche does not. As well as tolerating heat, this type of cream is a fine addition to a sauce or soup.

Which oil should you use for cooking? The market has so many options. We recommend canola oil for cooking (see more about cooking oils on page 292). You can also cook with olive oil, but only on medium heat. If the temperature is too high, over the oil's smoking point, fatty acids will develop, and the oil will change to an unhealthy state that has a negative effect on both flavor and nutritional value.

TOMATO SOUP WITH POACHED EGGS AND QUINOA SALAD

Tomato soup with egg is a fond- childhood memory for me and for many other Norwegians. Here's an updated and healthful version of this favorite dish. Quinoa salad substitutes for the bread and the eggs are poached, but the soup is almost unchanged.

SOUP

1 onion

3 garlic cloves

3 celery stalks

1 carrot, peeled

Canola oil

1 tablespoon tomato paste

5 cups (1.25 l) canned or boxed chopped tomatoes

3 tablespoons apple cider vinegar or white wine vinegar

1¾ cups (430 ml) water

Salt and cayenne pepper

Fresh organic lemon juice

⅓ cup (80 ml) olive oil

1 tablespoon honey

QUINOA SALAD

½ cup (105 g) quinoa

2 cups (375 g) cherry tomatoes

2 cups (60 g) lightly packed baby spinach

Salt and freshly ground pepper

2 tablespoons olive oil

Fresh organic lemon juice

POACHED EGGS

4 eggs

⅓ cup (80 ml) vinegar

Salt

SOUP

Chop the onion, garlic, celery, and carrot. Heat a little oil in a soup pot and sauté the chopped vegetables with the tomato paste. Add the canned tomatoes, vinegar, and water. Bring to a boil, reduce heat to a simmer, cover, and cook for 30 minutes. Season to taste with salt, cayenne, and a few drops of lemon juice. Stir in the olive oil and honey. Process in a blender and press through a sieve with the back of a large spoon. (You can omit straining the soup to preserve all the nutrients, but the soup will be thicker.) Set aside and keep warm.

QUINOA SALAD

Cook the quinoa in lightly salted water for 20–25 minutes. Drain in a fine-mesh sieve. In a salad bowl, combine the tomatoes and quinoa. Fold in the spinach. Season to taste with salt and pepper. Toss with the oil and a few drops of lemon juice.

POACHED EGGS

Crack each egg into a separate cup. In a wide shallow pan, bring 2 inches (5 cm) water to a rapid simmer. Stir in the vinegar and a sprinkle of salt. Remove the pan from the heat. While using a ladle to constantly swirl the water, pour one egg into the pan. Cook until the white is opaque, 2–3 minutes. Remove with a slotted spoon. Repeat to cook the remaining eggs.

Divide the salad among four soup bowls and top with a poached egg. Ladle the soup over.

LEFTOVERS?
USE THE SOUP AS A PASTA SAUCE OR A SAUCE FOR MEAT OR FISH.

CRISPY ONION TART WITH HERRING AND YOGURT DRESSING

The crispy base with caramelized onions complements the sour herring fillets in this dish, which reminds me of pizza.

TART
1 package (¼ oz/7 g) active dry yeast (2½ tsp)

1¼ cups (310 ml) lukewarm water

3 cups (375 g) white spelt flour

1¼ cups (155 g) whole-grain spelt flour

Salt and freshly ground pepper

4 red onions, sliced

4 yellow onions, sliced

YOGURT DRESSING
¾ cup (180 ml) plain Greek yogurt

1 teaspoon honey

2 garlic cloves, minced

2 tablespoons sour cream

Salt and cayenne pepper

Fresh organic lemon juice

14 ounces (440 g) pickled herring

4 cups (125 g) lightly packed mâche or baby lettuce leaves

Preheat the oven to 475°F (250°C).

TART
In a bowl, combine all the ingredients and stir until smooth. Cover the bowl with a kitchen towel and let the dough rest for 15 minutes. On a floured work surface, divide the dough into four pieces. Roll each piece of dough about ¼ inch (6 mm) thick. Fold a large piece of parchment paper in half and place on a baking sheet. Place the dough on top. Top the dough with the one-fourth of the onion slices, pressing them down a little into the dough. Sprinkle with salt and pepper. Repeat with the remaining dough and onions. Let the dough rest for 10 minutes and then bake until crisp, 15–20 minutes.

YOGURT DRESSING
Stir the yogurt, honey, garlic, and sour cream together in a bowl. Add salt, cayenne, and lemon juice to taste.

Cut the herring into bite-sized pieces. Divide the lettuce, herring, and yogurt dressing over the baked tarts.

You can find herring in various jars and boxes on the grocery shelves. Some herring fillets need to be rinsed in water or milk; others, such as pickled herring, can simply be dried off and used as is.

Capers are the flower buds of the caper bush.
They are sold either in brine or preserved with salt.
Capers are a first-class flavor intensifier, particularly
for dishes from southern Europe. A good substitute
is the pickled buds of wild garlic (ramps) flowers.

LEMON MACKEREL WITH CABBAGE AND GRILLED ASPARAGUS

This is a first-class summer dish: fresh mackerel, crisp cabbage, and asparagus.
It's both healthful and easy to make—what could be better?

⅓ cup (80 ml) olive oil

3 tablespoons capers

Grated zest and juice of 2 organic
lemons

1½ pounds (750 g) mackerel fillets

Salt and freshly ground pepper

Fresh parsley leaves and chopped
fresh chives

CABBAGE

¾ cup (90 g) walnuts

2 small pointed (sweetheart) or
napa cabbages

4 ounces (125 g) fresh white
goat cheese

Leaves from 3 sprigs fresh
tarragon, minced

3 tablespoons olive oil

Salt and freshly ground pepper

Fresh organic lemon juice

GRILLED ASPARAGUS

1 bunch green asparagus

3 tablespoons olive oil

Salt and freshly ground pepper

Fresh organic lemon juice

Preheat the oven to 200°F (95°C).

Pour the olive oil into a baking dish. Add the capers and lemon zest and juice. Rub the fish fillets with salt and pepper and place them in the pan. Cover the pan with aluminum foil. Bake in the oven for 10 minutes. Remove the foil. Sprinkle with parsley and chives.

CABBAGE

Toast the walnuts in a dry frying pan; empty into a bowl. Cut each cabbage in half lengthwise. Toast in the dry frying pan until the outside is almost burnt. Transfer the cabbage to a bowl. Crumble the cheese over the cabbage and add the walnuts. Sprinkle with the tarragon and drizzle with the olive oil. Season to taste with salt, pepper, and lemon juice.

GRILLED ASPARAGUS

Break off and discard the tough ends of the asparagus spears. Toast the asparagus in a dry frying pan until it takes on some color. Add the oil and season to taste with salt, pepper, and lemon juice.

Serve the mackerel with the cabbage and asparagus alongside.

LEFTOVERS?
PROCESS THE MACKEREL TO A PASTE TO SPREAD ON BREAD.

FISH CAKES WITH RAW VEGGIE SALAD

Here's a new method for making fish cakes: crisp, warm slices of bread are spread with fish paste and sautéed. Take the ingredients for the fish paste right from the refrigerator.

FISH PASTE

1 pound (500 g) white-fleshed fish fillets, chopped

Salt

1–2 eggs

⅓ cup (80 ml) heavy cream

⅓ cup (80 ml) whole milk

2 tablespoons minced fresh chives

Salt and freshly ground pepper

Fresh organic lemon juice

12 ounces (375 g) beets, trimmed and scrubbed

1 apple, cored and diced

2 tablespoons capers

1 tablespoon minced fresh parsley

¼ cup (60 ml) olive oil

Salt and freshly ground pepper

Fresh organic lemon juice

4 slices bread

2 tablespoons canola oil

RAW VEGGIE SALAD

2 carrots, peeled

1 small head broccoli

2 cups (60 g) lightly packed baby lettuce leaves

2 tablespoons olive oil

Salt and freshly ground pepper

Fresh organic lemon juice

FISH PASTE

Process the fish with the salt in a food processor until thick. Blend in the egg(s), cream, milk and chives until smooth. Season to taste with salt, pepper, and lemon juice.

Boil the beets in a pot of salted water to cover until tender. Peel the beets and cut into small pieces. In a bowl, combine the beets, apple, capers, and parsley. Toss with the olive oil and season to taste with salt, pepper, and lemon juice.

Spread the fish paste over the bread slices. Heat the canola oil in a frying pan and sauté, bread side down, until the bread is golden. Turn and sauté until the fish paste is cooked through.

RAW VEGGIE SALAD

Cut the carrots and broccoli into thin strips. In a bowl, combine the vegetables and toss with the oil. Season to taste with salt, pepper, and lemon juice. Top the fish cakes with the beet mixture and serve the salad alongside.

LEFTOVERS?

OMIT THE BREAD AND MAKE A COLD SALAD WITH THE REST OF THE INGREDIENTS. THE FISH CAKES ARE A GOOD ADDITION TO THE LUNCH BOX, ALONG WITH A TASTY RÉMOULADE, MUSTARD, AND A HANDFUL OF LETTUCE LEAVES.

While table salt (NaCl) contains only the mineral element natrium, sea salt contributes a whole spectrum: over eighty elements that our bodies and plants in nature both need.

BAKED POLLOCK WITH MARINATED VEGETABLES

For this dish, the fish is baked in the oven with the vegetables so that the flavors blend and nothing goes to waste. You can substitute halibut or lingcod for the pollock.

¾ cup (90 g) pearl barley, soaked overnight

Salt

1 bunch parsley, stemmed

1 garlic clove

Grated zest and juice of ½ organic lemon

¼ cup (60 ml) olive oil

MARINADE

Seeds of 1 vanilla bean

Grated zest of ½ organic lemon

½ teaspoon ground fennel

½ teaspoon ground coriander

3 tablespoons apple cider vinegar

1 tablespoon honey

⅓ cup (80 ml) olive oil

⅓ cup (80 ml) water

2 fennel bulbs, trimmed and cut into strips

8 ounces (250 g) spring carrots

2 red onions, sliced

4 sprigs fresh thyme

10 kale leaves or broccolini stalks

1 bunch green asparagus

1¼ pounds (625 g) pollock, halibut, or lingcod fillets, cut into large pieces

Salt

In a saucepan, simmer the barley in lightly salted water to cover until tender, 30–40 minutes; drain and let cool. In a blender, process the parsley with the garlic, then add the lemon zest, lemon juice, and oil and process until smooth. Fold into the cooked barley.

MARINADE

In a baking dish, combine all the ingredients for the marinade.

Preheat the oven to 350°F (180°C). Add the fennel strips, carrots, red onions, and thyme to the marinade. Cover with aluminum foil and bake for 15 minutes.

In a pot of lightly salted boiling water, cook the kale and asparagus for 4 minutes; drain, transfer to a bowl of ice water, and drain again. Sprinkle the fish fillets with salt. Remove the foil from the dish and add the fish, kale, and asparagus to the dish. Bake, uncovered, for 7–8 minutes.

Serve the fish and vegetables in the baking dish with the herbed barley alongside.

Pollock is a tasty fish that comes from Norwegian waters. Lingcod or halibut is a good substitute.

84

COD SALAD WITH QUINOA PANCAKES

This dish is not just exciting, but also healthful, so it's good all around.
Children like packing into a just-made pancake, especially if they don't know it's raw fish.

COD SALAD

8 celery stalks, thinly sliced

Juice of 5 limes

⅓ cup (80 ml) olive oil

1 head iceberg lettuce

1 pound (500 g) half-frozen cod or red snapper fillets, finely sliced

1 red onion, sliced

1 cucumber, cut into sticks

Salt and freshly ground pepper

2–3 tablespoons minced fresh tarragon (optional)

Minced fresh cilantro

AVOCADO CREAM

3 avocados, peeled and pitted

Juice of 3 limes

¼ cup (60 ml) water

⅓ cup (80 ml) olive oil

Salt and cayenne pepper

PANCAKES

1 cup (185 g) quinoa

2 tablespoons olive oil

2 egg yolks

¼ cup (60g) sour cream

½ cup (60 g) white spelt flour

Salt and freshly ground pepper

2 egg whites, beaten to soft peaks

COD SALAD

In a food processor, pulse the celery slices with the lime juice and oil to make a dressing. Shred the iceberg lettuce and spread on a wide platter. Top with the fish fillets, onion, and cucumber sticks. Drizzle with the dressing and season with salt and pepper. Garnish with tarragon, if using, and cilantro.

AVOCADO CREAM

In a blender, process the avocados, lime juice, and water. Add the oil and blend until smooth. Season to taste with salt and cayenne pepper.

PANCAKES

In a saucepan, simmer the quinoa in salted water to cover for 20 minutes, or until tender; drain. Process the quinoa, oil, egg yolks, and sour cream in a food processor. Add the flour and season to taste with salt and pepper. Pour into a bowl and fold in the beaten egg whites. Cook the pancakes in a dry frying pan.

Serve the pancakes along with the cod salad and avocado cream; let guests fill their own pancakes.

We recommend using half-frozen fish for this recipe, because they will be easier to cut into thin slices.

TROUT SALAD

This recipe is perfect for fresh and elegant dinner salad. Most of the elements of this dish can be prepared ahead of time and combined at the last minute.

4 trout fillets (1¼ lb/625 g total), skin on

Salt and freshly ground pepper

2 tablespoons olive oil

4 hearts of romaine lettuce

1 small head frisée

4 eggs

1 red onion, sliced

4 ounces (125 g) green beans, trimmed

1 can sardines, drained

MAYONNAISE

1 egg yolk

1 tablespoon mustard

1 tablespoon apple cider vinegar

Grated zest of 1 organic lemon

1¼ cups (310 ml) canola or olive oil

Salt and cayenne pepper

Fresh organic lemon juice

10 fresh dill sprigs

Nasturtium blossoms or other edible flowers (optional)

LEFTOVERS?
DISCARD ANY REMAINING FISH SKIN AND PACK THE SALAD FOR YOUR LUNCHBOX.

Preheat the oven to 250°F (120°C).

Scrape off any protruding scales from the trout skin. Sprinkle salt and pepper on both sides of each fillet and place the fish on a baking pan. Drizzle with olive oil. Bake the fish for 20 minutes. Remove the fish from the oven and peel off the skin. Increase the temperature to 400°F (200°C). Line a baking sheet with parchment paper and lay the fish skin on it. Bake until crisp, 10 minutes. While you wait, prepare the rest of the salad ingredients: Tear the greens into small pieces and arrange on a wide platter. Boil the eggs for 6 minutes, rinse under cold running water, peel, and cut in half crosswise. Crumble the fish skin and divide it over the greens with the fish fillets. Slice the onion and sprinkle it over the salad. Steam the green beans in a steamer for 3–4 minutes and rinse to cool. Spread the beans over the salad and top with the sardines.

MAYONNAISE
Whisk the egg yolk with the mustard and vinegar in a bowl. Add the lemon zest. Add the oil in a thin drizzle while whisking constantly. Season to taste with salt, cayenne pepper, and lemon juice; adjust the flavoring with lemon juice. Use a spoon to dollop mayonnaise onto the salad. Garnish the salad with dill sprigs and, if desired, nasturtium flowers to serve.

Steaming vegetables until tender in a steamer over lightly salted water allows the vegetables to retain their nutritional value, flavor, texture, and color.

SUNCHOKE SOUP WITH SMOKED MACKEREL

Look for knobbly tan-colored sunchokes (also called Jerusalem artichokes) in the produce section and use this sweet, nutty tuber to add flavor and texture to savory dishes.

SOUP

1 pound (500 g) unpeeled sunchokes

2 tablespoons canola oil

2 shallots, minced

2 cups (500 ml) whole milk

1¾ cups (430 ml) water

¾ cup (185 g) sour cream

⅓ cup (80 ml) olive oil

Salt and cayenne pepper

Fresh organic lemon juice

BAKED SUNCHOKES

8 ounces (250 g) unpeeled sunchokes

1–2 tablespoons olive oil

Salt

½ cup (75 g) hazelnuts, coarsely chopped

8 ounces (250 g) smoked mackerel, skinned, boned, and cut into small pieces

1 cup (30 g) lightly packed mâche or baby lettuce leaves

SOUP

Cut the sunchokes into large pieces. Heat the canola oil in a frying pan and sauté the sunchoke pieces and shallots until the shallots are translucent. Add the milk and water. Cover and cook until the sunchokes are tender, 30–40 minutes. In a blender or food processor or with a stick blender, process the mixture until smooth. Blend in the sour cream and olive oil. Season to taste with salt, cayenne pepper, and a few drops of lemon juice. Strain the soup through a sieve. (You can omit straining the soup to preserve nutrients, but the soup will be thicker.)

BAKED SUNCHOKES

Preheat the oven to 400°F (200°F). Cut the sunchokes into large pieces. Put them in a baking dish and toss them with oil. Season with salt. Bake until tender, about 30 minutes. Stir in the hazelnuts and mackerel pieces.

Serve a good helping of the baked sunchokes with the nuts and mackerel in warm soup bowls. Pour the soup over and garnish with mâche.

LEFTOVERS?

YOU CAN USE THIS SOUP AS A SAUCE TO SERVE WITH FISH OR SHELLFISH.

Sunchokes are a good substitute for potatoes. Even though they have a delicious sweetness, they won't affect your blood sugar the way the starch in potatoes does because the sweetness in sunchokes comes from the indigestible fiber inulin. It tastes good and is beneficial for digestion, but is not absorbed by the body. Sunchokes can also be eaten raw.

FISH BALLS IN WHITE SAUCE

Making your own fish balls means this dish will be as fresh as possible
and full of flavor. You will hardly be able to wait to make this recipe again.

FISH BALLS

1 pound (500 g) white-fleshed fish
    fillets, such as pollock, halibut,
    or lingcod, cut into small pieces

1–2 eggs

⅓ cup (80 ml) heavy cream

⅓ cup (80 ml) whole milk

Salt

Pinch of cayenne pepper

Grated zest of 1 organic lemon

4 cups (1 l) cold water

1 pound (500 g) unpeeled
    Yukon gold potatoes

WHITE SAUCE

¼ cup (60 g) butter

½ cup (60 g) white spelt flour

⅓ cup (80 ml) heavy cream

2 leeks, white part only, sliced
    and rinsed

2 carrots, peeled and sliced

Salt and cayenne pepper

Fresh organic lemon juice

4 ounces (125 g) shelled shrimp

Minced fresh chives and
    fresh parsley

2 tablespoons grated horseradish

FISH BALLS

In a food processor, blend all the ingredients for the fish balls until smooth. (If using a blender, process the ingredients in increments.) Dampen your hands and roll about 2 tablespoonfuls of the mixture to form each fish ball, or use two spoons to shape it Fill a saucepan with the water, bring to a rapid simmer, and add the fish. Cook the fish balls for 10–12 minutes; do not let the water boil. When the fish balls are cooked, they will pop up to the surface. Using a slotted spoon, transfer the fish balls to a plate, reserving and keeping warm about 4 cups (1 l) of the cooking liquid for the sauce.

Boil the potatoes in a saucepan of lightly salted water until tender, about 30 minutes. Drain.

WHITE SAUCE

Melt the butter in a saucepan. Stir in the flour, then the reserved warm cooking liquid and cream. Bring to a boil. Add the leeks and carrots and cook for 8–10 minutes, or until the sauce is thickened, the vegetables are tender, and the raw taste of flour has disappeared. Season to taste with salt, cayenne pepper, and a few drops of lemon juice.

Stir the fish balls into the sauce to warm them up. Stir in the boiled potatoes. Add the shrimp. Sprinkle generously with the herbs. Sprinkle the horseradish on top and serve.

For this dish, we recommend
sustainable wild fish.

BAKED COD WITH CREAMED CABBAGE AND CRISP BACON

The consistency of this fish dish is almost like cream. If a winter depression threatens, this dish is sure to chase it away.

½ cup (75 g) pearl barley, soaked overnight

Salt

4 cod or red snapper fillets (1¼ lb/625 g total)

2 tablespoons olive oil

WHITE SAUCE

2 tablespoons butter

3 heaping tablespoons white spelt flour

2 cups (500 ml) whole milk

3 tablespoons sour cream

Fresh organic lemon juice

Cayenne pepper

PICKLED ONIONS

1¼ cups (300 ml) water

⅓ cup (80 ml) apple cider vinegar

⅓ cup (80 ml) honey

1 large red onion, sliced

4 small yellow onions, sliced

1 small head cabbage, cored and cut into shreds

8 kale leaves, chopped

3 slices bacon

Garden cress or watercress sprigs

Preheat the oven to 350°F (180°C).

In a saucepan, simmer the barley in salted water to cover for 30–40 minutes, or until tender; drain.

While the barley cooks, rub the fillets with salt and drizzle with oil. Place the fish on a baking pan and bake until opaque throughout, 12–15 minutes.

WHITE SAUCE

Melt the butter in a saucepan. Stir in the flour and then add the milk and sour cream, stirring until the mixture is smooth. Cook for about 10 minutes or until the taste of raw flour has disappeared. Season to taste with lemon juice and cayenne pepper.

PICKLED ONIONS

Combine the water and vinegar in a nonreactive saucepan and bring to a boil. Add the honey and remove from the heat. Cook the red and yellow onions in a saucepan of lightly salted simmering water until tender. Drain and add to the vinegar mixture. Let cool. Store, covered, in the refrigerator for up to 1 week.

Cook the cabbage and kale in a saucepan of lightly salted simmering water to cover until tender, 7–8 minutes (or 10–15 minutes in a steamer). Drain. Stir the drained cabbage and kale into the white sauce with the barley. Cut the bacon into small pieces and fry in a dry frying pan until crisp. Pour the cabbage mixture into a bowl. Shred the cooked cod with a fork and sprinkle over the cabbage mixture. Garnish with bacon and watercress and serve with pickled onions alongside.

Onions can vary in size from a tennis ball to a golf ball. Roughly calculated, 4 small yellow or red onions equal 1 large onion. The beneficial bacteria in our digestive tracts love onions of every type, from spring onions and leeks to shallots and red onions. Onions contribute to a good balance of intestinal flora and have the power to protect against many types of illness.

LINGCOD, SQUASH, AND SUNCHOKE CASSEROLE

Here's a dinner that's ready in a jiffy. Just cut up the vegetables, mix, and bake in a warm oven. The fish can be done at the last minute.

1 pound (500 g) acorn or butternut squash, peeled and seeded

1 pound (500 g) unpeeled sunchokes

1 onion

8 garlic cloves

6 tablespoons olive oil

Salt and freshly ground pepper

Fresh organic lemon juice

6 sprigs fresh rosemary

1¼ pound (625 g) lingcod or other white-fleshed fish, cut into large pieces

5 slices bacon, cut into strips

Preheat the oven to 400°F (200°C).

Cut the squash into small pieces. Cut the sunchokes into pieces if they are rather large. Cut the onion into wedges. Add the squash, sunchokes, onion, and garlic to a baking dish and toss with the oil. Season with salt, pepper, and lemon juice, then stir in the rosemary. Roast for 20 minutes. Place the fish pieces on top of the vegetables in the dish for the last 7–8 minutes of the roasting time. In a dry frying pan, fry the bacon until crisp while the vegetables bake. Garnish the casserole with the crisp bacon and serve.

LEFTOVERS?
HEAT IN A COVERED PAN ON LOW HEAT.

Sunchokes can be stored, but over time the peel thickens and the structure of the flesh becomes coarser. Older sunchokes need a longer cooking time than fresh ones picked early in the season; you may want to peel them.

FISH GRATIN WITH BROCCOLINI SALAD

Impossible to make this favorite dish in time for dinner, you think? Try it!

1 pound (500 g) unpeeled
   fingerling potatoes

1¼ cups (310 ml) whole milk

2 garlic cloves

1 pound (500 g) salt cod fillets,
   skinned

5 eggs, separated

3 tablespoons olive oil

Salt and cayenne pepper

HERB OIL

1 garlic clove

¼ cup (60 ml) olive oil

Handful of fresh basil leaves

¼ cup (60 ml) canola oil

1 cup (125 g) grated Parmesan
   cheese

BROCCOLINI SALAD

8 stalks broccolini or broccoli

3½ oz (105 g) roasted peppers
   (from a jar), finely chopped

½ tablespoon chopped anchovies

½ tablespoon capers, drained

3 tablespoons olive oil

1 tablespoon fresh organic
   lemon juice

Preheat the oven to 400°F (200°C).

Dice the potatoes. Pour the milk into a saucepan, add the potatoes and garlic, and cook until tender. Dice the fish fillets. Stir into the potatoes and milk and steep for 4–5 minutes. Drain, reserving the milk for another use. In a food processor, pulse the fish and potatoes until coarsely blended. Add the egg yolks and olive oil and blend well. Beat the egg whites in a large bowl until soft peaks form and fold into the mixture. Season with salt and cayenne pepper. Pour into a greased baking dish. Bake for 20–25 minutes, or until the top is golden.

HERB OIL

Process the garlic, olive oil, and basil in a blender while you drizzle in the canola oil. Finish by folding in the Parmesan cheese.

BROCCOLINI SALAD

In a saucepan, boil the broccolini in salted water to cover just until tender, 4–5 minutes. Dry well and then toast in a dry frying pan. For the dressing, combine the roasted peppers, anchovies, capers, olive oil, and lemon juice in a bowl. Coat the warm broccolini in the dressing.

Drizzle the herb oil over the gratin and serve in the baking dish, with the salad alongside.

This herb oil makes an excellent salad dressing, and it can also be spread on bread slices. It will last for a few days in the refrigerator.

POACHED PLAICE IN CREAMED MUSSEL SOUP

Here's a soup that comes in handy when you are in a hurry for an everyday feast. It's a complete meal that tastes ever so good. The most time-consuming part of the process is preparing the fish.

1 cup (125 g) pearl barley, soaked overnight

Salt

1 pound (500 g) mussels, rinsed

2 celery stalks, sliced

1 onion, coarsely chopped

1 garlic clove, minced

1 bay leaf

1 stalk lemongrass, white part only, peeled, or grated zest of 1 organic lemon

¼ cup (60 ml) apple cider vinegar

¾ cup (180 ml) water

¾ cup (185 g) cold butter, diced

Cayenne pepper

Fresh organic lemon juice

1 pound (500 g) plaice or other flatfish, cut into bite-sized pieces

4 plum tomatoes, cut into wedges

Chopped fresh chives

Cook the pearl barley in a saucepan of lightly salted boiling water for 30–40 minutes; drain

In a soup pot, combine the mussels with the celery, onion, garlic, bay leaf, lemongrass, vinegar, and water. Bring to a boil, cover, and cook for 5–6 minutes, or until the mussels open. Uncover and strain the soup stock into a large saucepan. Whisk the diced butter into the soup stock and season to taste with salt, cayenne pepper, and a few drops of lemon juice. Add the fish pieces to the soup. Let simmer for 3–4 minutes; the soup should not come to a boil. Add the mussels, vegetables, barley, and tomato wedges and heat until warmed through. Garnish with chives.

LEFTOVERS?
USE THE SOUP AS A SAUCE FOR SEAFOOD PASTA.

Mussels taste fantastic. The stock from cooking mussels makes the best base for soups and sauces with seafood.

HALIBUT SOUS VIDE

Cooking sous vide was, for a long time, a cooking method used mainly in high-end restaurants. Because this method maintains both flavor and consistency and preserves nutritional value, it has garnered a much larger public now that small sous vide machines have become available for the home. Investing in one will make your everyday life happier and tastier.

PARSLEY BUTTER

½ cup (125 g) + 1 tablespoon butter, at room temperature

1 garlic clove, minced

2 tablespoons minced fresh parsley

Salt and cayenne pepper

Fresh organic lemon juice

4 halibut fillets (1¼ lb/625 g total)

1 cup (125 g) pearl barley, soaked overnight

Salt and freshly ground pepper

4 ounces (125 g) turnips

1 bunch green onions

1 bunch radishes

6 ounces (185 g) small carrots or large carrots cut into sticks

Grated zest of 1 orange and 1 organic lemon

2 sprigs fresh tarragon

6 tablespoons (90 ml) olive oil

¼ cup (60 ml) water

Juice of ½ organic lemon

Chopped fresh parsley

PARSLEY BUTTER

In a bowl, whip the butter and then add the garlic and parsley. Season with salt, cayenne pepper, and lemon juice. Spread the butter over the fish fillets before sealing each in its own vacuum bag.

In a saucepan, cook the pearl barley in salted boiling water to cover for 30–40 minutes, or until tender; drain. Parboil the vegetables in a saucepan of salted water for 2–3 minutes. Add the vegetables and barley to a vacuum bag together with the citrus zests, tarragon, oil, and water. Season with salt, pepper, and lemon juice. Seal the bag. Heat the water in a sous vide machine or pot to 160°F (70°C) and cook the bag for 25 minutes. During the last 8–9 minutes of the cooking time, add the fish bags to the water, so everything will be ready at the same time. Arrange the vegetables and then the fish on a large platter. Garnish with parsley.

CUSK WITH TOMATOES AND BEANS

Fresh cusk is one of the best fish for cooking.
Its meat is rather dense but also moist, and its flavor is mild.

1 cup (220 g) dried white beans,
  soaked overnight

1 whole head garlic, halved
  crosswise

2 onions, sliced

6 sprigs fresh tarragon

Zest of 1 organic lemon

Juice of ½ organic lemon

⅓ cup (80 ml) olive oil

1¼ cups (310 ml) water

2 cups (375 g) cherry tomatoes

2 cups (60 g) lightly packed
  baby spinach

1¼ pounds (625 g) cusk fillets or
  other white-fleshed fish, cut into
  large chunks

Stale bread, torn

Chopped fresh parsley

4 anchovies

Mayonnaise for serving (page 42)

Preheat the oven to 350°F (180°C).

In a baking dish, combine the beans, garlic, onions, tarragon, lemon zest and juice, oil, and water. Cover and bake for 45 minutes, or until the beans are tender. Remove from the oven, add the tomatoes, fold in the spinach, and place the fish on top. Bake for another 10 minutes. Toast in the oven until crisp and golden, 8–10 minutes. Sprinkle the bread, parsley, and anchovies on top of the casserole. Serve with homemade mayonnaise.

Small, fatty fish, such as anchovies, sardines, and herring naturally have a high amount of omega-3 fatty acids, which contribute to physical and psychological health, concentration, and memory. With anchovy fillets preserved in extra-virgin olive oil, you get the benefits of omega-9s. Anchovies also have selenium, which activates our own antioxidants, and calcium for good muscle function plus strong teeth and bones.

Trout is a fatty fish and an important source of vitamin D and omega-3s. The trout and salmon sold in grocery stores are often farm-raised. Because farm-raised fish do not eat food that is natural for them, they don't generate the same amount of smart building blocks for the body that wild fish do. For that reason, buy wild fish when you can.

SALT-BAKED TROUT WITH CREAMED MUSHROOMS AND SALAD

This is a variation on the classic trout with butter sauce.
The butter is still here but is mixed in with the vegetables.
The fish is cooked in the oven, making it extra moist.

1 lime

6 sprigs fresh tarragon

1¾ pounds (875 g) trout fillets, skin on

2 tablespoons olive oil

½ cup (125 g) coarse salt

CREAMED MUSHROOMS

½ cup (90 g) quinoa

8 ounces (250 g) assorted mushrooms

2 tablespoons canola oil

2 shallots, minced

1 cup (250 ml) heavy cream

Salt and freshly ground pepper

Fresh organic lemon juice

2 tablespoons minced fresh chives

MUSTARD DRESSING

2½ tablespoons Dijon mustard

1½ tablespoons honey

2 tablespoons apple cider vinegar

⅔ cup (160 ml) olive oil

Salt and freshly ground pepper

Fresh organic lemon juice

2 cups (60 g) lightly packed mixed lettuces

Preheat the oven to 350°F (180°C).

Slice the lime and arrange the slices on the bottom of a baking dish. Place the tarragon on top of the lime. Top with the fish fillets, skin side up. Drizzle the fish fillets with the olive oil and coat the skin of the fish with coarse salt. Bake the fish for 13–15 minutes. Remove the skin before serving.

CREAMED MUSHROOMS

Cook the quinoa in a saucepan of simmering lightly salted water to cover until tender, 20–30 minutes; drain. Cut the mushrooms into bite-sized pieces. In a frying pan, heat the oil and sauté the mushrooms and shallots until softened, about 2 minutes. Pour in the cream and cook for 8–10 minutes, or until the mixture thickens as for a cream sauce. Stir in the quinoa. Season to taste with salt, pepper, and lemon juice. Garnish with chives.

MUSTARD DRESSING

In a bowl, whisk the mustard with the honey and vinegar. Whisk in the oil. Season to taste with salt, pepper, and lemon juice.

Tear the lettuce leaves into smaller pieces and toss in a bowl with the dressing. Serve alongside the fish and the creamed mushrooms.

LEFTOVERS?

FLAKE THE FISH INTO SMALLER PIECES AND MIX WITH LETTUCE AND YOUR FAVORITE VEGGIES.

HERRING SALAD WITH POTATO PANCAKES

This is fancy fast food. You can take the herring right out of the jar, and the pancakes can be made in no time. There is definitely something to the expression, "Eating herring makes you kind."

DRESSING

⅓ cup (90 g) sour cream

¼ cup (60 g) organic cottage cheese

2 tablespoons olive oil

2 teaspoons coarse mustard

1 teaspoon honey

Grated zest of ½ organic lemon

POTATO PANCAKES

1¼ pounds (625 g) unpeeled fingerling potatoes, cut into small pieces

1 egg

1 onion, finely chopped

Salt and freshly ground pepper

3–4 tablespoons canola oil

HERRING SALAD

6 eggs

2 cups (60 g) lightly packed baby spinach

14 ounces (440 g) sour herring

3 slices bacon, diced

DRESSING

Well ahead of serving time, mix all the ingredients in a bowl and let stand at room temperature.

POTATO PANCAKES

In a food processor, pulse the potatoes until mashed. Add the egg. Stir in the onion. Season with salt and pepper. Form into thin pancakes. In a large frying pan, heat the oil and cook the pancakes until crispy. Set aside and keep warm.

HERRING SALAD

Boil the eggs for 8–9 minutes. Rinse under cold water and then peel. Put the spinach in a bowl and add the herring. Chop the egg whites and crumble the yolks. Add the chopped whites to the bowl with the dressing; toss to coat. Fry the bacon in a dry frying pan until crisp.

For each serving, top a potato pancake with the herring salad and sprinkle with the bacon and crumbled egg yolks.

Most of the nutrition in potatoes is found in the skin. Prepare potatoes with the peel on but wash them carefully first. It's best to choose small potatoes, so you'll get the most possible skin in relation to the starchy inside.

FISH CAKES WITH CREAMED VEGGIES

I love to make fish dishes, and homemade fish cakes taste so much better than packaged ones. The children like fish cakes with root vegetables so there are seldom any leftovers.

CREAMED VEGETABLES

⅔ cup (100 g) pearl barley, soaked overnight

Salt

¼ cup (60 g) butter

½ cup (60 g) white spelt flour

4 cups (1 l) milk

1 cauliflower, trimmed and cut into florets

1 broccoli, cut into florets

3 carrots, peeled and sliced

Cayenne pepper

Fresh organic lemon juice

1 pound (500 g) hake or haddock, skinned, boned, and chopped

1 teaspoon salt

1 large or 2 small eggs

¾ cup (180 ml) milk

Grated zest of ½ organic lemon

Fresh organic lemon juice

Cayenne pepper

2–3 tablespoons olive oil

Chopped fresh chives

CREAMED VEGETABLES

In a saucepan, cook the pearl barley in lightly salted simmering water until tender, 30–40 minutes; drain. In another saucepan, melt the butter; add the flour and slowly stir in the milk until the mixture thickens to a sauce. Cook for 10 minutes, stirring constantly.

Boil the vegetables in a saucepan of salted water or steam until tender; drain. Add the vegetables and barley to the sauce. Season to taste with salt, cayenne pepper, and lemon juice.

Serve the creamed vegetables on a large platter and top with the fish cakes. Garnish with chopped chives.

In a food processor, pulse the fish with the salt into a paste. Add the egg and milk. Season with lemon zest and juice and cayenne pepper. Use a spoon to shape the fish cakes. In a frying pan, fry them in the oil until golden. Set aside and keep warm.

LEFTOVERS?

IF YOU'RE MAKING FISH SOUP, YOU CAN ADD THE FISH CAKES AND VEGETABLES JUST BEFORE SERVING. THE CREAMED VEGETABLES WILL MAKE THE SOUP SMOOTHER.

Dry ingredients such as grains, groats, lentils, rice, and beans absorb water as they cook. As a rule, the volume of these ingredients doubles when they are cooked; ½ cup (100 grams) dried lentils becomes approximately 1 cup (200 grams) when cooked.

A cooking technique the French call *en papillote* works well for almost all types of seafood. A tight paper packet helps preserve both flavor and nutritional elements.

You will find many nutrition-rich rice substitutes among these recipes. Try whole-grain spelt, barley, millet, and oats. If you are gluten-sensitive, or just want more variety, you might try quinoa, amaranth, buckwheat, and brown rice. Don't forget that whole grains must be soaked overnight to break down the phytic acid that can irritate the intestines and limit the absorption of nutrients from the food. Soaking also shortens the cooking time a little, which, in turn, helps to preserve nutrients. You can freeze already soaked grain so you'll have some ready to cook.

FISH BAKED IN PARCHMENT

With the help of parchment paper and a little kitchen twine, you can make packets
of fish and vegetables to bake in the oven. The result is extra-moist fish.

⅔ cup (100 g) spelt grains or
pearl barley, soaked overnight

Salt

LEMON BUTTER
⅔ cup (155 g) butter,
at room temperature

Grated zest and juice of
½ organic lemon

Salt and cayenne pepper

Minced fresh dill or fennel fronds

ASPARAGUS SALAD
2 bunches green asparagus

½ cup (80 g) pine nuts

⅓ cup (80 ml) olive oil

Salt and freshly ground pepper

Fresh organic lemon juice

2 tablespoons goat-milk
cream cheese

2 tablespoons sour cream

Salt and freshly ground pepper

Minced fresh basil

½ Savoy cabbage, cored
and cut into fine strips

1 fennel bulb, trimmed and
cut into strips

1¼ pounds (625 g) cusk or
other white-fleshed fish,
cut into 4 pieces

4 cups (450 g) cherry tomatoes,
halved

Boil the grains in a saucepan of lightly salted water until tender, 30–40 minutes; drain.

Preheat the oven to 350°F (180°C). Cut eight 12 x 12 squares of parchment paper.

LEMON BUTTER
In a bowl, whip the butter with the lemon zest and juice. Season to taste with salt and cayenne pepper and fold in the dill.

ASPARAGUS SALAD
Break off the tough ends of the asparagus. Sauté or toast the spears in a frying pan until tender, 8–10 minutes. Toast the pine nuts in a dry frying pan until fragrant annd golden. In a blender, grind the nuts and oil to a paste. Coat the asparagus with the paste. Season with salt, pepper, and lemon juice. Blend the cheese and sour cream in a bowl and season to taste with salt and pepper. Spoon the cheese over the asparagus and garnish with chopped basil.

Layer 2 squares of parchment paper on a work surface and mound one-fourth of the cabbage and fennel strips in the center. Top with one-fourth of the spelt and a piece of fish. Dollop with lemon butter. Add one-fourth of the tomatoes. Fold the sheets of paper together to make a snug packet and tie closed with twine. Repeat to make 4 packets. Place the packets in a baking dish. Bake for 15–20 minutes and serve right from the packets.

Serve each packet alongside a portion of the asparagus salad.

POLLOCK WITH POTATOES AND EGGS

This is a fine way to serve a fish dinner, especially if you have children who claim they don't like fish.

1¼ pounds (625 g) upeeled fingerling potatoes

1¼ pounds (625 g) pollock, halibut, or lingcod

Salt

1 tablespoon olive oil

EGGS

4 eggs

¾ cup (185 g) + 2 tablespoons butter

1 leek, white part only, sliced and rinsed

Garden cress or watercress sprigs

8 carrots, peeled

2 apples, cored

Juice of ½ organic lemon

Preheat the oven to 350°F (180°C).

Boil the potatoes in a saucepan of lightly salted water until tender. Drain and let them dry in the cooking pot. Lightly mash the potatoes with a fork. Place the fish on a buttered baking pan. Sprinkle with salt. Drizzle the oil over. Cover with aluminum foil and bake for 6–7 minutes, or until the fish is opaque throughout.

EGGS

Boil the eggs for 7–8 minutes. Rinse under cold running water. Peel the eggs and mash them in a bowl. Melt the butter in a frying pan and cook the eggs and leek over medium-low heat until the leek is translucent. Stir in the mashed potatoes.

Arrange the fish on top of the eggs and potatoes. Garnish with garden cress.

Chop the carrots and apples. Fold in the lemon juice and serve alongside the fish, eggs, and potatoes.

COOKING TIP

Add a little olive oil to servings of raw fruit and vegetables. This allows the body to absorb more of the nutrients in the food.

LEFTOVERS?

FISH IN WHITE SAUCE IS A TIMELESS FAVORITE.

Pollock is a sustainable wild fish in Norway. Children who "don't like fish," like pollock because its flavor is a little different. The best part is that it's in season year-round! If you can't find it in your market, substitute halibut, lingcod, or another white-fleshed fish.

FISH GRATIN WITH LENTILS, CABBAGE, AND CARROTS

This filling gratin of vegetables and cod makes a complete meal.

CHEESE SAUCE

3 tablespoons butter

¼ cup (30 g) white spelt flour

1 cup (250 ml) whole milk

¾ cup (90 g) freshly grated
   Parmesan cheese

1¼ pounds (625 g) cod or halibut
   fillets

Salt and freshly ground pepper

1¼ pounds (625 g) carrots
   (about 10), peeled

Salt and freshly ground pepper

Olive oil

½ cup (105 g) French green lentils,
   rinsed

4 slices bacon, cut into strips

1 pointed (sweetheart) cabbage
   or small napa cabage,
   cut into strips

Salt and cayenne pepper

Fresh organic lemon juice

Preheat the oven to 350°F (180°C).

CHEESE SAUCE

Melt the butter in a saucepan; stir in the flour and then slowly whisk in the milk. Stir in the Parmesan. Bring to a simmer and cook, whisking frequently, for 10 minutes.

Divide the fish into 4 pieces. Place the fish in a baking dish and sprinkle with salt and pepper. Pour the cheese sauce over the fish and set aside. Spread the carrots on a baking pan. Add the salt, pepper, and olive oil; turn to coat. Bake the carrots for 20–25 minutes, or until they are very tender. After 10 minutes, transfer the fish to the oven and bake for 8–10 minutes. Cook the lentils in a saucepan of lightly salted boiling water for 20 minutes, or until tender; drain. While the fish and carrots finish baking, fry the bacon in a frying pan until crispy. Add the cabbage and sauté for 3–4 minutes, or until the cabbage is tender. Stir in the lentils and carrots and then season to taste with salt, cayenne pepper, and lemon juice.

Serve in the baking dish.

Lentils are sometimes called "poor man's protein." They contribute valuable plant protein to meals, as do vegetables from the cabbage family (such as broccoli, cauliflower, kale, and Brussels sprouts), other legumes (peas and beans), nuts, and seeds. Even if a plant food doesn't contribute all the essential amino acids, the combination of different plant foods will give you everything you need. Grain products, for example, contain lysine, while legumes have methionine. If you combine legumes and grains in your food for the day, you do not need to eat them at the same meal.

ICEBERG LETTUCE WITH SMOKED MACKEREL AND SUNCHOKE WAFFLES

Everybody loves waffles. This meal lifts waffles to new heights for both taste and nutrition. Sunchokes complement the distinctive flavor of mackerel and the mild lettuce leaves.

MAYONNAISE

1 egg yolk

1 tablespoon mustard

1 tablespoon apple cider vinegar

1¼ cups (310 ml) canola oil

Salt and cayenne pepper

Fresh organic lemon juice

SALAD

1 large head iceberg lettuce

4 smoked mackerel fillets

1 red onion, half chopped, half sliced

2 apples, cored; 1 diced and 1 cut into julienne

Salt and freshly ground pepper

Fresh organic lemon juice

Minced fresh dill, parsley, or chervil

SUNCHOKE WAFFLES (MAKES 10)

8 ounces (250 g) unpeeled sunchokes, chopped

1¾ cups (430 ml) whole milk

2 eggs

1 cup (250 ml) buttermilk

3 cups (375 g) white spelt flour

1 teaspoon baking powder

⅔ cup (5155 g) butter, melted

MAYONNAISE

In a bowl, whisk the egg yolk with the mustard and vinegar. Slowly drizzle in the oil, whisking constantly until the mixture is thoroughly blended and airy. Season with salt, cayenne pepper, and a few drops of lemon juice.

SALAD

Remove the outer lettuce leaves and arrange on a tray as lettuce "bowls." Chop the heart of the lettuce and blend with the mayonnaise, fish pieces, chopped onion, and diced apple. Season to taste with salt, pepper, and lemon juice. Spoon the mixture into the lettuce bowls. Garnish with the red onion slices, julienned apple, and dill.

SUNCHOKE WAFFLES

In a saucepan, boil the sunchokes in the milk until tender. Process in a blender or food processor. Add the remaining ingredients and process until smooth. Cook in a waffle iron just before serving.

Serve the waffles alongside the lettuce bowls of salad.

LEFTOVERS?

REMOVE THE LETTUCE LEAVES AND PULSE THE FISH MIXTURE TO A PASTE IN A FOOD PROCESSOR. SPREAD THE PASTE ON YOUR BREAKFAST BREAD.

Mackerel and herring are nutritious fish
that you could eat often. Studies show that mackerel
has surprisingly few environmental poisons (dioxins)
in its flesh compared to other fatty fish.

BAKED TROUT WITH TZATZIKI AND GREEK SALAD

All together: trout, Greek salad, pearl barley, and creamy cucumber salad. Healthful and good.

TZATZIKI

2–3 cucumbers

¾ cup (180 ml) plain Greek yogurt

2 garlic cloves

⅓ cup (90 ml) sour cream

Salt

Fresh organic lemon juice

GREEK SALAD

⅔ cup (100 g) pearl barley, soaked overnight

Salt and freshly ground pepper

1 large cauliflower, trimmed

2 tablespoons canola oil

4 shallots, minced

⅓ cup (50 g) diced feta cheese

⅓ cup (50 g) black olives, pitted

3 tablespoons olive oil

Minced fresh cilantro

4 trout fillets (1¼ lb/625 g total), skin on

Salt and freshly ground pepper

Fresh organic lemon juice

Olive oil

Coarse salt

TZATZIKI

Cut each cucumber in half lengthwise. Use a teaspoon to scoop out the seeds. Slice the "shells." In a blender or food processor, process the yogurt and garlic. Add the sour cream and blend until smooth. Season to taste with salt and lemon juice. Fold in the cucumber slices.

GREEK SALAD

Cook the pearl barley in a saucepan of lightly salted boiling water until tender, 30–40 minutes; drain. Separate the cauliflower florets all the way in to the stalk. Heat the canola oil in a frying pan and sauté the cauliflower and shallots until tender and golden. Stir in the barley, feta cheese, olives, and olive oil. Season to taste with salt and pepper. Garnish with cilantro.

Preheat the oven to 350°F (180°C).

Sprinkle the fish with salt, pepper, and lemon juice. Oil a baking dish with the olive oil and place the fish in the dish skin side up. Bake for 8–10 minutes, or until tender. Peel off the skin. Sprinkle with salt and a few drops of lemon juice to serve.

Serve the fish in the baking dish, alongside the tzatziki and the salad.

LEFTOVERS?

FILL THICK POTATO PANCAKES WITH THE LEFTOVERS OR USE STURDY LETTUCE OR CABBAGE LEAVES AS WRAPS

Real cream, butter, and yogurt have a fat content that is important for flavor. Minimally processed dairy products, used sparingly, can provide an array of building blocks for good health. Whole milk has only 3 percent fat, with more than 400 different beneficial fatty acids.

Umami is called the fifth taste. Some also refer to it as the "meat taste." The four other tastes are salt, sour, sweet, and bitter. Umami is found in foods that are rich in the amino acid glutamate, such as sun-dried tomatoes. Umami was discovered about one hundred years ago by Kikunae Ikeda, a Japanese professor, when he isolated a flavor substance in seaweed soup that he could not identify. Glutamate, which is bound to proteins, does not produce a umami taste until processed; a food must be ripened, fermented, preserved, or heated for the glutamate to shine forth as the satisfying taste of umami. Other umami foods are miso, nori seaweed, ripe cheese, green tea, anchovies, and mushrooms.

TOMATO-SEAFOOD CASSEROLE

Everyone knows how the conversation with children goes when you want them to try a new food. Fish and shellfish can be a challenge. This Provençal-style seafood casserole has a satisfying tomato flavor that makes it easy to like.

AÏOLI

1 egg yolk

1 tablespoon apple cider vinegar

1 tablespoon mustard

1¼ cups (310 ml) olive oil

Salt and cayenne pepper

Fresh organic lemon juice

2 garlic cloves, minced

CASSEROLE

14 ounces (400 g) cusk or other white-fleshed fish

1 fennel bulb, trimmed and sliced (reserve fronds)

2 celery stalks, sliced

1 red chile, minced

2 garlic cloves, minced

1 onion, sliced

⅓ cup (80 ml) olive oil

1 pound (500 g) mussels, rinsed

1¾ cups (430 ml) water

3 tablespoons apple cider vinegar

3½ cups (600 g) canned or boxed chopped tomatoes

Salt and cayenne pepper

Fresh organic lemon juice

Bread for serving

AÏOLI

Whisk the egg yolk with the vinegar and mustard. Whisk as you pour in the oil in a thin drizzle until the aïoli is airy and completely blended. Season with salt, cayenne pepper, and a few drops of lemon juice. Stir in the garlic. Set aside.

Preheat the oven to 350°F (180°C).

CASSEROLE

Cut the fish into small pieces. In a wide ovenproof pot, sauté the vegetables in the olive oil. Add the mussels and then the water, vinegar, and tomatoes. Boil for 5 minutes. Add the fish pieces. Cover the pot and transfer it to the oven. Bake for 5–6 minutes. Season to taste with salt, cayenne pepper, and lemon juice. Transfer the pot to the table and remove the lid. Garnish with the reserved fennel fronds. Serve with aïoli and bread.

COOKING TIP

If you harvest wild mussels, look for posted warnings at the beach and check online to make sure no poisonous algae is blooming along your stretch of coastline. Otherwise, buy farmed mussels at the fish counter.

LEFTOVERS?

USE THE LEFTOVERS AS A PASTA SAUCE.

HONEY-GLAZED PORK

All the flavors are preserved in this dish. Enjoy making pork sandwiches
with any leftovers—everyone will be jealous.

SALAD

⅔ cup (90 g) oat groats, soaked
  overnight

¾ cup (90 g) walnuts

1 apple, cored and diced

3 cups (90 g) lightly packed baby
  spinach

¼ cup (60 ml) olive oil

Salt and freshly ground pepper

Fresh organic lemon juice

2 pounds (1 kg) baby carrots or
  carrot slices

2 tablespoons olive oil

Salt and freshly ground pepper

1½ pounds (750 g) boneless
  pork shoulder

3 tablespoons honey

20 fresh sage leaves

CREAM CHEESE

⅓ cup (90 g) cream cheese

2 tablespoons heavy cream

Salt and freshly ground pepper

Fresh organic lemon juice

Minced fresh chervil for garnish

SALAD

Cook the oat groats in a saucepan of lightly salted boiling water until
tender, 30–40 minutes; drain. Coarsely chop the walnuts. In a bowl,
combine the apple and the spinach. Stir in the cooked oats, oil, and nuts.
Season to taste with salt, pepper, and a few drops of lemon juice.

Position a rack in the center of the oven. Preheat the oven to 400°F
(200°C).

In a bowl, toss the carrots with the olive oil. Season with salt and
pepper. Pour the carrots onto a baking pan and roast for 25–30 minutes,
or until tender. Remove the carrots and keep them warm until serving.
Cut the pork into 20 slices. Season with salt and pepper. Turn on the
broiler. Lay the pork slices on a broiler pan, brush each pork slice with
honey, and place a sage leaf on each slice. Broil until golden and crisp,
10–15 minutes.

CREAM CHEESE

In a bowl, mix the cheese with the cream. Season to taste with salt,
pepper, and lemon juice.

Drop dollops of cream cheese over the carrots and sprinkle with chervil.
Serve with the pork slices and salad.

Bees blend nectar with their own saliva to make naturally thick honey. The different plants they take the nectar from affect both the consistency and taste. Fructose-rich honeys, such as acacia, are thinner than other honeys. Too much fructose is transformed into unhealthful fat in the blood. An excessive intake of fructose can actually make the liver fat. If you want runny honey, simply place a jar of local raw honey in a pan of 105°F (40°C) water. It will then be runny but have much more nutritional value than refined, filtered honey. Save the latter for cooking, as heating honey above 95°F (35°C) destroys the natural enzymes in raw honey.

GROUND BEEF WITH BEANS

This take on chili con carne is full of good nutrition. The best thing is that
you can blend in all the vegetables that aren't the children's favorites.
If you follow the recipe, even the youngest will lick their plates clean.

2 red chiles, seeded

2 carrots, peeled

1 fennel bulb, trimmed

1 onion

4 garlic cloves

2 tablespoons canola oil

1¼ pounds (625 g) ground beef

2 tablespoons tomato paste

About 2 cups (185 ml) canned or
  boxed chopped tomatoes

1 star anise pod

1 tablespoon ground cumin

¾ cup (180 ml) water

½ cup (105 g) dried white beans,
  soaked overnight

½ cup (105 g) dried black beans,
  soaked overnight

5 ounces (155 g) fresh green
  beans, trimmed

Salt and cayenne pepper

⅓ cup (80 ml) sour cream

Fresh cilantro sprigs

Leaves from 1 head iceberg lettuce

2 tablespoons extra-virgin olive oil

1 teaspoon fresh lemon juice

Chop the vegetables. In a large frying pan, heat the oil and sauté the vegetables with the ground beef and tomato paste until the vegetables are golden. Stir in the tomatoes, anise, cumin, and water. Pour into a saucepan, cover, and simmer for 45 minutes. Cook the soaked beans in salted water to cover until tender, about 40 minutes; drain.

Meanwhile, in a large bowl, mix together the olive oil and lemon juice. Tear the lettuce leaves into pieces, toss in the olive oil and lemon juice dressing, and set aside for serving. Parboil the green beans in a saucepan of lightly salted water for 2–3 minutes. Add the white, black, and green beans to the meat mixture. Cook for another 3–5 minutes, or until everything is heated through. Season to taste with salt and cayenne pepper. Drop dollops of sour cream over the casserole and garnish with cilantro. Serve with the salad alongside.

Serve your guests only the best heavy cream or sour cream. Real cream provides energy and is full of important nutritional elements. If you can, choose organic heavy cream or sour cream. Choose crème fraîche for cooking, as it won't separate when heated.

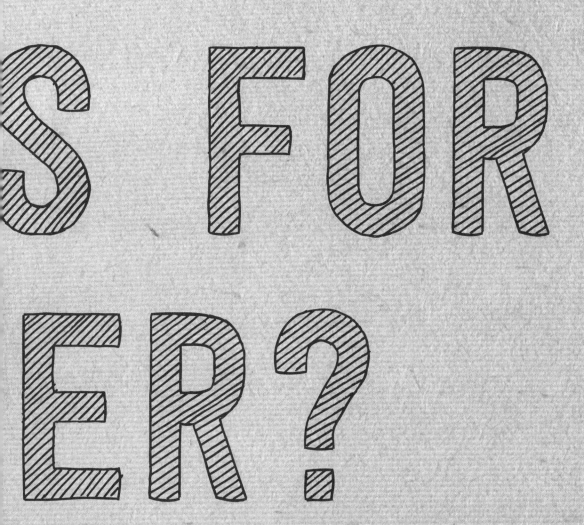

WILD GAME STEW

Wild meat is fantastically good. It's lean, which makes for a clean and mild flavor.
It also has healthy fatty acids because wild animals eat the plant foods that are natural for them,
and their meat is also rich in omega-3 (ALA). The nutritional statistics for wild game
are close to those for fish. A bacon spread on flatbread fills out the flavor picture.

1¼ pounds (625 g) venison, reindeer, or moose "plum" (darkest thigh meat)

3 tablespoons canola oil

1 onion, diced, or 8 ounces (250 g) pearl onions

2 garlic cloves, coarsely chopped

1 bay leaf

1 teaspoon black peppercorns

⅔ cup (100 g) spelt grains or pearl barley, soaked overnight

3 carrots

1 small celery root

4 celery stalks

½ small head cabbage, cored and chopped

1 bunch kale, stemmed and rinsed

Salt and freshly ground pepper

Fresh organic lemon juice

BACON SANDWICHES

3 slices bacon, diced

⅔ cup (155 g) butter, at room temperature

Salt and freshly ground pepper

Fresh organic lemon juice

Flatbread, homemade (page 184) or store-bought

Cut the meat into large dice. In a large frying pan, sauté the meat in oil with the onion and garlic until everything takes on color. Add the bay leaf, peppercorns, and water to cover. Cover and cook until the meat is tender, 45–50 minutes. Cook the spelt grains in a saucepan of lightly salted boiling water until tender, 20–30 minutes. Peel the carrots, celery root, and celery and cut into large dice. Cut the kale into crosswise shreds. When the meat has 7–8 minutes remaining, add the vegetables, including the cabbage. When the vegetables are cooked, add the spelt and season to taste with salt, pepper, and lemon juice.

BACON SANDWICHES

In a dry frying pan, fry the bacon until crisp; using a slotted spoon, transfer to paper towels to drain. Beat the butter in a deep bowl until pale in color. Stir in the bacon. Season to taste with salt, pepper, and lemon juice. Spread on flatbread. Serve the sandwiches alongside the stew.

Kale is available almost all year. It is a valuable member of the cabbage family that can used for many different dishes. It may be the healthiest vegetable you can eat. You can make kale chips by tearing the leaves into large pieces (discard the stems), coating with olive oil and sea salt, and toasting for 8–10 minutes on a baking sheet in the center of a preheated 350°F (175°C) oven. These are a super substitute for potato chips at everyday meals.

CHICKEN DRUMSTICKS IN TOMATO SAUCE

Drumsticks are one of my favorite parts of the chicken.
In this dish, the moist chicken meat adds flavor to the sauce and vice versa.
And the oven does most of the work for you.

BARLEY SALAD

⅔ cup (100 g) pearl barley, soaked overnight

Salt and freshly ground pepper

2 fennel bulbs, trimmed

2–3 tablespoons olive oil

Fresh organic lemon juice

MARINADE

⅓ cup (80 ml) honey

2 onions, sliced

¼ cup (30 g) grated fresh ginger

1 chile, minced

6 garlic cloves, chopped

¼ cup (60 ml) apple cider vinegar

2 cans or boxes (28 oz/875 g each) chopped tomatoes

½ cup (250 ml) olive oil

Salt and cayenne pepper

Salt and freshly ground pepper

1¾ pounds (875 g) chicken drumsticks or chicken thighs

Coarsely chopped fresh parsley

BARLEY SALAD

Cook the barley in a saucepan of lightly salted water until tender, 30–40 minutes. Drain and let cool. Sliver the fennel with a cheese slicer. In a bowl, combine the barley and fennel and stir in the olive oil. Season to taste with salt, pepper, and a few drops of lemon juice.

Preheat the oven to 400°F (200°C).

MARINADE

Melt the honey in a stockpot and add the onions, ginger, chile, and garlic. Pour in the vinegar and tomatoes. Bring to a boil, reduce to a simmer, and cook for 5–6 minutes. Stir in the olive oil. Season to taste with salt and cayenne pepper.

Sprinkle salt and pepper over the chicken pieces and put the chicken in a baking dish. Pour the marinade over the chicken. Bake the chicken for 20–30 minutes. Garnish with parsley and serve with the barley salad alongside.

LEFTOVERS? SERVE SLICED CHICKEN WITH A TOMATO SALAD.

Canned and boxed plum tomatoes have been ripened on the vine , where they develop more taste and color before being harvested. They are also full of healthful nutrients.

WARM ASIAN SALAD WITH BEEF

This salad brings out the best in the vegetables. Instead of being stir-fried, they are coated with bouillon to preserve their freshness. You'll find most of the ingredients in Asian groceries, and you can substitute chicken or fish for the beef.

1¼ pounds (625 g) sirloin steak

Salt and freshly ground pepper

Canola oil

½ cup (105 g) dried white beans, soaked overnight

4 cups (1 l) water

⅓ cup (50 g) coarsely chopped fresh ginger

1 stalk lemongrass, white part only, peeled and chopped

1 red chile, minced

2 garlic cloves, chopped

2 kaffir lime leaves

⅓ cup (80 ml) olive oil

1 white or purple cauliflower

1 bunch green asparagus

4 heads bok choy, separated into leaves

2 avocados, peeled, pitted, and diced

2 tablespoons sesame seeds, toasted

3 tablespoons olive oil

2 tablespoons soy sauce

Fresh lime juice

Salt and freshly ground pepper

Mizuna leaves for garnish

Minced fresh cilantro

2 limes, halved

Preheat the oven to 350°F (180°C).

Rub the meat with salt and pepper. In an ovenproof frying pan, brown the meat on all sides in the canola oil. Transfer the pan to the oven and bake the meat for 15–20 minutes, depending on how done you like your beef. Let the meat cool for 15 minutes before slicing; reserve the pan.

Drain and rinse the beans well. In a large saucepan, combine the beans, water, ginger, lemongrass, chile, garlic, kaffir lime leaves, and olive oil. Bring to a boil, reduce to a simmer, and cook the beans until tender, about 40 minutes. While the beans cook, divide the cauliflower into florets. Break off the tough ends of the asparagus and discard them. Cut the spears into small lengths. Rinse the bok choy.

Remove the beans from the water with a slotted spoon. Cook the cauliflower and asparagus in the bean-cooking water for 4–5 minutes. Add the bok choy for the last 2 minutes of cooking. On a large platter, arrange the beans and vegetables on the bottom and the meat slices on top. Sprinkle the avocado pieces over the salad. In a bowl, mix the sesame seeds with the olive oil and soy sauce. Season to taste with lime juice, salt, and pepper. Drizzle the dressing over the salad. Top with mizuna leaves and cilantro.

Serve with limes that have been quickly sautéed in the reserved pan.

You can buy fresh and dried herbs in grocery stores year-round. Fresh herbs will add something extra to both the flavor and presentation of most dishes. You can also grow your own herbs to enjoy. Some herbs have antioxidants equivalent in power to a pound (500 g) of fruit. But fruit can load the body with too much natural sugar, while herbs offer delightful flavor and healthful benefits. Eat some fresh herbs and sprouts every day!

MEATBALLS IN ONION SAUCE

Meatballs are often served in a smooth brown sauce,
but these are served in a satisfyingly chunky onion sauce.

ONION SAUCE

¼ cup (60 ml) olive oil

5 yellow onions, sliced

1 cup (125 g) pearl onions or
    shallots

⅓ cup (80 ml) vinegar

2 tablespoons honey

⅓ cup (80 ml) water

3 bay leaves

⅔ cup (155 g) French green lentils

Salt and freshly ground pepper

MEATBALLS

1¼ pounds (625 g) ground beef

Salt and freshly ground pepper

1 teaspoon baking powder

1 egg, beaten

⅓ cup (80 ml) water

3 shallots, minced

3 tablespoons canola oil

1 pound (500 g) green peas

14 ounces (440 g) fresh or frozen
    lingonberries, red currants,
    or cranberries

⅓ cup (80 ml) honey

ONION SAUCE

Heat the oil in a frying pan and sauté the yellow onions and pearl onions until golden. Stir in the vinegar and honey. Thin with the water and add the bay leaves. Stir in the lentils and cook, uncovered, until the lentils are tender, about 20 minutes. Season to taste with salt and pepper.

MEATBALLS

Put the meat in a bowl, season with salt and pepper, add the baking powder and work in by hand; work in the egg and then thin with the water. Stir in the shallots. Dampen your hands to shape the mixture into balls or use a spoon. In a frying pan, heat the oil and cook the meatballs.

Transfer the meatballs to the onion sauce and add the green peas. Let the mixture stand for 5 minutes. In a food processor, pulse the berries with the honey. Serve right from the pan, with a side of lingonberries.

LEFTOVERS?

PROCESS THE ONION SAUCE IN A BLENDER OR FOOD PROCESSOR AND THIN WITH WATER IF NEEDED. ADD THE LEFTOVERS AND SERVE AS A STEW.

Frozen peas retain their flavor,
appearance, and nutritional value.

Using sweeteners in cooking contributes to a good taste experience. Try the many different flavors of honey, from mild to intense, depending on what kind of flowers the nectar was gathered from.

CHICKEN WINGS WITH CAESAR SALAD

Caesar salad is a classic. It's common now to add chicken to this salad.
Here, you get two favorite dishes, salad and chicken wings,
that complement each other nutritionally.

CHICKEN WINGS

12 small turnips or radishes

3 pounds (1.5 kg) chicken wings

2 tablespoons minced fresh
   tarragon

1 red chile, seeded and minced

2 garlic cloves

1 tablespoon honey

2 tablespoons olive oil

Juice of ½ organic lemon

Salt and freshly ground pepper

3 slices bacon

3 slices bread

CAESAR DRESSING AND SALAD

1 egg yolk

1 tablespoon mustard

1 tablespoon apple cider vinegar

¾ cup (180 ml) olive oil

1 garlic clove, minced

¼ cup (125 ml) sour cream

2 teaspoons Worcestershire sauce

Juice of ½ organic lemon

Salt and cayenne pepper

Leaves from 2 large heads
   romaine lettuce, torn

4 anchovy fillets

½ cup (60 g) shredded Parmesan
   cheese

Preheat the oven to 425°F (220°C).

CHICKEN WINGS

Cut the turnips into 2 or 4 pieces. Put them in a large bowl with the chicken wings. Mix in all the remaining ingredients for the chicken. Spread the mixture in a large baking dish and bake for 30–35 minutes.

Place the bacon on a baking pan lined with parchment paper. Tear the bread slices into pieces and spread them on the pan with the bacon. Toast in the oven for 10 minutes, or until crispy. Let cool on paper towels.

CAESAR DRESSING AND SALAD

Make the salad dressing by whisking the egg yolk, mustard, and vinegar in a bowl. Slowly drizzle in the olive oil, whisking all the time. Stir in the garlic, sour cream, Worcestershire sauce, and lemon juice. Season with salt and cayenne pepper. Toss the lettuce leaves with the dressing. Crumble the bacon and croutons and sprinkle over the salad. Arrange the anchovies on top and then add the Parmesan. Serve with the chicken wings alongside.

LEFTOVERS?

PICK THE MEAT OFF THE COOKED CHICKEN WINGS. ROMAINE LETTUCE IS SO DURABLE THAT LEFTOVER SALAD CAN EASILY BE KEPT IN THE REFRIGERATOR FOR A COUPLE OF DAYS.

CALF LIVER WITH MASHED POTATOES

Calf liver is a delicacy with a rich history in Norwegian cooking. Not only is it healthy, it also tastes wonderful if given the necessary respect during preparation.

1¼ pounds (625 g) calf liver

¼ cup (30 g) white spelt flour

3 tablespoons canola oil

Salt and freshly ground pepper

12 ounces (375 g) brussels sprouts

2–3 tablespoons butter

4 unpeeled apples,
  cored and sliced

1 tablespoon honey

Fresh organic lemon juice

MASHED POTATOES

1¼ pounds (625 g) unpeeled
  fingerling potatoes

⅓ cup (90 g) butter

1 cup (250 ml) whole milk

⅓ cup (80 ml) plain Greek yogurt

Salt and cayenne pepper

1¼ cups (155 g) fresh or frozen
  lingonberries, red currants,
  or cranberries

¾ cup (90g) blueberries

3 tablespoons honey

Minced fresh parsley

Cut the liver into equal-sized pieces about 1½ inches (4 cm) thick. Dip them in flour and brush off any excess flour. Heat the oil in a frying pan until it bubbles. Add the liver pieces and brown them on both sides. Lower the heat and fry 2–3 minutes more. Transfer the liver to a platter and keep warm. Season with salt and pepper. Trim the brussels sprouts, reserving the outer leaves to use as a garnish. Bring lightly salted water to boil in a saucepan and parboil the brussels sprouts for 4–5 minutes. Using a slotted spoon, transfer the sprouts to ice water to cool briefly. Drain and dry the brussels sprouts on paper towels. Cut each in half lengthwise. Melt the butter in the pan. Fry the apples with the brussels sprouts, the honey, and a little lemon juice.

MASHED POTATOES

In a stockpot, boil the potatoes in unsalted water until tender. Drain and let the potatoes dry by shaking in the pan over low heat before mashing the potatoes with the butter, milk, and yogurt. Season to taste with salt and cayenne pepper.

Mix the lingonberries and blueberries with the honey. Arrange the calf liver, brussels sprouts, and apple slices on heated plates. Garnish with the reserved brussels sprout leaves and parsley. Distribute the berries over the meat. Serve with the mashed potatoes.

LEFTOVERS?
HEAT A LITTLE CREAM AND ADD THE LEFTOVER VEGETABLES AND DICED LIVER FOR A TASTY LUNCH.

You can find liver in butcher shops and in the freezer section of markets year-round. It is both lean and protein-rich and has very high amounts of iron and folic acid (B9). Additionally, you'll get high doses of vitamin A, vitamin D, B12, phosphorus, zinc, and selenium. Don't overdo it because liver can also contain heavy metals. The flavors of calf liver, pork liver, and chicken liver are similar, so one can be substituted for the other.

LAMB AND VEGETABLE SOUP

This is a dinner you can make while you tidy up the place,
set the table, and still have a few minutes to catch up. The only thing you need
to think about during the preparation is that the vegetables need be cut into
equal-sized pieces so they will all be ready at the same time.

1½ pounds (750 g) boned lamb shoulder

6 cups (1.5 l) water

1 bay leaf

5 black peppercorns

1 cup (125 g) spelt grains, soaked overnight

1 leek, white part only, sliced and rinsed

3 carrots, peeled

8 ounces (250 g) green beans, trimmed

1 onion

1 celery stalk

2 cups (310 g) green peas

Fresh parsley sprigs

Olive oil

Dice the meat. In a soup pot, bring the water to boil with the bay leaf and peppercorns. Add the diced meat, cover, and simmer until tender, 40–50 minutes. Using a slotted spoon, transfer the meat to a bowl and reserve the pot and cooking water.

Cook the spelt grains in a saucepan of simmering salted water until tender, about 40 minutes; drain. Cut the leek, carrots, green beans, onion, and celery into small pieces and add to the cooking water in the reserved pot along with the peas. Stir in the cooked spelt grains. Add the cooked meat to warm and heat through. Serve in warmed soup bowls. Garnish with parsley and a drizzling of olive oil.

LEFTOVERS?
LAMB HASH IS A TRADITIONAL NORWEGIAN DISH.

Norwegian lamb is world-class meat. Sheep that graze in nature eat plants and herbs that give the meat beneficial fatty acids and a wonderful flavor. This kind of meat can yield almost double the amount of omega-3 fatty acids and smart conjugated linoleic acid (CLA) as the meat of sheep that don't graze. These fatty acids can strengthen the immune system, curb inflammation, make strong bones, better regulate blood sugar, and build stronger muscle mass. Talk about a bonus from a flavorful meat!

SAUSAGE AND EGG HASH

In general, this dish is made with leftovers. However, if you read this recipe, you'll find this is a new kind of hash. Pick a sausage with the highest amount of pure meat possible and with no or few additives.

1¼ pounds (625 g) pork sausages

2 tablespoons canola oil

4 celery stalks, sliced

8 ounces (250 g) Chinese long beans (asparagus beans), cut into 2-inch (5 cm) lengths

10 slices bread, preferably white spelt bread

1 whole head garlic, unpeeled

2 red onions, sliced

7 ounces (220 g) roasted peppers (from a jar), cut into strips

¼ cup (60 ml) olive oil

Salt and freshly ground pepper

6–8 eggs

2 tablespoons minced fresh parsley

Preheat the oven to 350°F (180°C).

Fry the sausages in the canola oil in a frying pan, then cut them into slices. Parboil the celery and beans in a saucepan of lightly salted water for a couple of minutes; drain. Coarsely tear the bread. Cut the garlic bulb in half crosswise and loosen the cloves. Combine the sausages, celery, beans, bread, garlic, onion, and pepper strips in a baking dish. Toss with the olive oil and sprinkle with salt and pepper. Make 6–8 depressions in the hash for the eggs. Crack the eggs one by one and slide each into a depression. Bake for 12–15 minutes, or until the eggs have set. Garnish with parsley and serve.

LEFTOVERS?
HEAT THE HASH UP OR EAT COLD.

Bell peppers become sweeter in flavor when they are roasted or grilled with the skin on, then peeled. You can buy peeled roasted peppers in a jar. This is one of the few vegetables that takes well to canning. Like tomatoes, red peppers contain lycopene, which is more easily absorbed by the body if the vegetables have been cooked. Usually vegetables lose some of their vitamin content when heated, so eat both raw and cooked vegetables every day.

CHICKEN FRICASSEE

This is a simple dish and a good way to vary the preparation of chicken breasts.
The sauce gives the dish a wonderful flavor of chicken, onion, tomatoes, and mushrooms.

⅔ cup (105 g) pearl barley, soaked overnight

1¼ pounds (625 g) boneless chicken breasts, skin on

Salt and freshly ground pepper

4 tablespoons (60 g) butter

1¼ cups (310 ml) heavy cream

1 onion, chopped

½ pound (250 g) mushrooms, sliced

Fresh organic lemon juice

4 plum tomatoes, cut into wedges

Fresh basil leaves

Cook the pearl barley in a saucepan of salted simmering water until tender, 30–40 minutes; drain.

Preheat the oven to 350°F (180°C).

Season the chicken pieces with salt and pepper on both sides. In an ovenproof frying pan, melt 2 tablespoons of the butter and sauté the chicken, skin side down, until golden and crisp. Turn the chicken pieces over and stir in half of the cream. Bake for 10 minutes, or until the chicken is cooked through. Transfer the chicken to a plate and reserve the drippings.

Melt the remaining 2 tablespoons butter in a saucepan and sauté the onion until tender. Add the mushrooms and cook until golden. Stir in the rest of the cream and the pan drippings. Cook until reduced by one-third. Season the sauce to taste with salt, pepper, and lemon juice.

Slice the chicken and add to the sauce with the barley and tomatoes. Top with the basil leaves and a few grinds of pepper.

LEFTOVERS?
REHEAT OVER LOW HEAT.

PORK CHOPS WITH BEETS AND PICKLED MUSHROOMS

I have a weakness for pork chops. I also love mushrooms and beets.
What could be more natural than to combine all three favorites in one dish?

BEETS

1 pound (500 g) beets, trimmed

6–7 tablespoons sour cream

2 tablespoons grated horseradish

PICKLED MUSHROOMS

1¼ cups (310 ml) water

⅓ cup (80 ml) apple cider vinegar

⅓ cup (80 ml) honey

Salt

1 red onion, sliced

1 pound (500 g) mixed mushrooms,
cut into bite-sized pieces

Salt

PORK CHOPS

4 pork chops (1¼ lb/625 g total)

Salt and freshly ground pepper

2 tablespoons canola oil

4 garlic cloves

3 sprigs fresh thyme

Fresh organic lemon juice

¼ cup (60 ml) water

½ cup (75 g) toasted and
skinned hazelnuts

Pinch of salt

½ garlic clove

⅓ cup (80 ml) olive oil

Fresh organic lemon juice

5 cups (155 g) lightly packed
baby lettuce leaves

Scrub the beets. Cook the beets in a saucepan of salted boiling water for 30–40 minutes. Drain and peel. Coarsely mash the beets in a bowl, using a fork. Transfer to a serving dish. Top with dollops of sour cream and grated horseradish.

PICKLED MUSHROOMS

In a saucepan, bring the water and vinegar to a boil and then add the honey. Season with salt. In a separate pan, parboil the onion slices and mushroom pieces for 3–4 minutes. Drain and transfer to the warm pickling brine. Pour into a sterilized glass jar. The pickled vegetables can be stored in the refrigerator for a long time.

Preheat the oven to 350°F (180°C).

PORK CHOPS

Season the meat with salt and pepper on both sides. Heat the oil in an ovenproof frying pan and cook the chops for 2 minutes on each side, or until golden brown. Add the garlic, thyme, a few drops of lemon juice, and the water. Transfer the pan to the oven and bake the chops for 8–12 minutes. Transfer to a platter and pour the pan juices over.

Crush the nuts, salt, and garlic with the olive oil in a mortar or blender. Add a few drops of lemon juice. Serve the dressing alongside the lettuce.

LEFTOVERS?
SERVE AS A PORK CASSEROLE WITH MUSHROOMS.

Horseradish is Scandinavia's aromatic alternative to pepper. It is especially good in dishes that combine dairy products with fish and meat. Fresh horseradish will keep longer if refrigerated. If you can't find fresh horseradish, buy some in a tube. Add freshly grated horseradish gradually to food because its strong flavor isn't immediately apparent.

CABBAGE ROLLS

Cabbage rolls are far from the first choice for an everyday meal when the family is in a hurry. However, you can happily make this traditional dish if you coordinate the work well. The flavor will be just as good today as it was in grandmother's time.

1 large green cabbage

Salt

FILLING

⅔ cup (100 g) spelt grains or pearl barley, soaked overnight

Salt and freshly ground pepper

1 pound (500 g) finely ground pork

1 egg, beaten

½ onion, finely chopped

STEW

4 tablespoons (60 g) butter

8 ounces (250 g) chanterelles or other mushrooms

Salt and freshly ground pepper

3 tablespoons white spelt flour

1¾ cups (400 ml) whole milk

Cayenne pepper

5 kale leaves, stemmed and coarsely chopped

2 tablespoons chopped fresh parsley

Preheat the oven to 350°F (180°C).

Tear off 8 of the outermost cabbage leaves (two per person). Boil the leaves in a saucepan of salted water to cover until tender, 5–6 minutes. Using tongs, transfer to paper towels to drain. Cut the remaining cabbage into shreds for the stew.

FILLING

Simmer the spelt grains in a saucepan of lightly salted water until tender, 30–40 minutes; drain. Work the salt and pepper into the ground pork with your hands. Work in the egg, onion, and spelt grains. Divide the filling among the cabbage leaves. Fold into rolled packets and place in a baking dish, seam side down. Fill the dish with water to cover by ⅜ inch (1 cm). Cover with aluminum foil. Bake for 20–25 minutes. Uncover and drain off the cooking liquid, reserving ¼ cup (60 ml) for the stew.

STEW

In a frying pan, melt 2 tablespoons of the butter and fry the mushrooms until tender. Season with salt and pepper. Melt the remaining 2 tablespoons butter in a saucepan. Stir in the flour and then add the milk; cook until the sauce is smooth, about 10 minutes. Stir in the reserved cooking liquid. Season to taste with salt and cayenne pepper. Pour half of the mushrooms and all of the kale and shredded cabbage into the stew and cook for 2–3 minutes. Garnish with the remaining mushrooms and parsley and serve.

LEFTOVERS?

CAREFULLY HEAT THE CABBAGE ROLLS IN THE OVEN IN A COVERED PAN WITH A LITTLE WATER.

In principle, anything can be used to fill cabbage rolls because the adaptable flavor of cabbage goes well with most fillings. Use your imagination and combine the flavors you like best.

LAMB GRATIN WITH PROVENÇAL TOMATOES

When you look through this recipe, doesn't it remind you of something you've eaten before? Yes, it's a version of the British shepherd's pie. In this recipe, sunchokes add flavor and texture to the lamb.

3 carrots, peeled

1 onion

2 garlic cloves

¼ cup (60 ml) canola oil

1¾ pounds (875 g) ground lamb

1 tablespoon tomato paste

2¼ cups (440 g) canned or boxed chopped tomatoes

⅓ cup (80 ml) water

2 bay leaves

Salt and cayenne pepper

2 tablespoons butter

3 tablespoons white spelt flour

2 cups (500 ml) whole milk

Salt and cayenne pepper

8–10 unpeeled sunchokes

3 tablespoons fresh white goat cheese

Leaves from 3 sprigs fresh rosemary

TOMATO SALAD

3 cups (644 g) halved cherry tomatoes

1 garlic clove

¾ cup (90 g) walnuts

¾ cup (90 g) grated Parmesan cheese

Juice of ½ organic lemon

⅓ cup (80 ml) olive oil

Fresh basil leaves

Preheat the oven to 400°F (200°C).

Coarsely chop the carrots, onion, and garlic. Heat the oil in an ovenproof frying pan over high heat and sauté the lamb for 3–4 minutes. Stir in the the carrots, onion, and garlic and cook until tender, about 5 minutes. Stir in the tomato paste and cook for a few more minutes. Stir in the tomatoes, water, and bay leaves. Cook the sauce for 25 minutes. Season to taste with salt and cayenne pepper. Pour into a baking dish.

Melt the butter in a saucepan. Stir in the flour and then gradually whisk in the milk until the sauce is smooth. Simmer the sauce for 10 minutes. Season to taste with salt and cayenne pepper. Pour the white sauce over the lamb mixture.

Cut the sunchokes into thin slices. Arrange a layer over the top of the white sauce. Sprinkle goat cheese on top. Garnish with rosemary. Bake for 20 minutes.

TOMATO SALAD

Put the tomatoes in a baking dish. In a blender, grind the garlic, walnuts, and Parmesan. Blend in the lemon juice and olive oil. Stir into the tomatoes. During the last 10 minutes of baking the lamb, put the tomatoes in the oven and bake for 10 minutes. Sprinkle basil leaves over the tomatoes to serve.

LEFTOVERS?

MORE LEFT IN THE PAN THAN YOUR GUESTS COULD EAT? HEAT THE LEFTOVERS IN A COVERED PAN IN A PREHEATED 300°F (150°C) OVEN.

As long as sunchokes are in season, you should leave the peel on to preserve the flavor and save the nutrients. The longer it is stored the thicker the peel becomes and should be removed. Sunchokes can be used raw in salads, but drizzle a little lemon juice over the surface after peeling and cutting, or they will turn brown. Sunchokes don't have starch, but they do have the carbohydrate inulin, which is not absorbed by the body, so they are the perfect substitute for potatoes if you are diabetic. They contribute to stable blood sugar and also replenish minerals such as potassium, calcium, phosphorus, and iron.

GAME MEAT PATTIES WITH MUSHROOMS, BRUSSELS SPROUTS, AND LINGONBERRIES

You can use whatever kind of game meat you like with this recipe; ground beef or buffalo could also substitute. The tougher cuts of game meat can be minced or ground. Since game meat is lean, it is important to add some fat, such as heavy cream, to the patties.

⅓ cup (50 g) pearl barley, soaked overnight

Salt and freshly ground pepper

1¼ pounds (625 g) ground venison, moose, or reindeer

7 slices bacon, finely chopped

1 egg, beaten

⅔ cup (160 ml) heavy cream

1 onion, finely chopped

1 tablespoon minced fresh rosemary

2 tablespoons canola oil

MUSHROOM SALAD

12 ounces (375 g) brussels sprouts

Salt and freshly ground pepper

6 ounces (185 g) chanterelles or other mushrooms

Canola oil

1 onion, coarsely chopped

1 cup (125 g) fresh or frozen lingonberries, red currants, or cranberries

1 tablespoon honey

¼ cup (60 ml) water

1 large pear, cored

3 tablespoons olive oil

Fresh parsley sprigs

Cook the barley in a saucepan of lightly salted boiling water until tender, 30–40 minutes; drain.

Preheat the oven to 350°F (180°C).

In a bowl, mix the meat and bacon by hand. Season with salt and work into the meat and then add the pepper. Work in the egg and then the cream. Blend in the onion, rosemary, and cooked barley. Form 8 meat patties with wet hands or two spoons. In an ovenproof frying pan, heat the canola oil and brown the patties on both sides. Bake in the oven for about 10 minutes.

MUSHROOM SALAD

Trim the brussels sprouts, reserving the outer leaves to use as a garnish. In a saucepan, cook the brussels sprouts in salted boiling water until tender, 3–4 minutes. (To preserve more of the nutrients, steam them in a steamer—it will take a little more time than boiling.) Drain and cool briefly in ice water; drain again.

Cut the mushrooms into chunks. In a frying pan, heat the oil and sauté the mushrooms and onion. Transfer to a bowl and season with salt and pepper. In another bowl, macerate the lingonberries in the honey and water for 7–10 minutes. Peel the pear and slice it into thin slivers with a cheese slicer. Fold the pear slices into the warm salad together with the olive oil, brussels sprouts, and macerated lingonberries. Garnish with parsley and the reserved brussels sprout leaves. Serve the salad alongside the patties.

LEFTOVERS?
COLD PATTIES TASTE GOOD.

PORK STEW WITH TOMATOES AND MASHED POTATOES

To enhance the flavor of the pork, I added chorizo sausage to this stew.
The chile flavors in the sausage harmonize well with the mild pork.

1¾ pounds (875 g) boned
  pork shoulder

3 tablespoons canola oil

10 shallots, coarsely sliced

8 garlic cloves, coarsely sliced

2 tablespoons tomato paste

1 red chile, seeded and minced

4 ounces (125 g) smoked (Spanish)
  chorizo sausage, sliced

2 cans or boxes (15 oz/470 g each)
  chopped tomatoes

2 bay leaves

5 ounces (155 g) roasted peppers
  (from a jar)

Salt and cayenne pepper

Fresh parsley leaves

MASHED POTATOES

1¼ pounds (625 g) unpeeled
  fingerling potatoes

¾ cup (180 ml) whole milk

⅔ cup (160 ml) sour cream

Salt

Dice the meat. In a large soup pot, brown the meat in the oil with the shallots and garlic. Add the tomato paste, chile, and chorizo and continue to cook until everything has taken on more color. Add the tomatoes, bay leaves, and water to cover. Cover and cook until the meat is tender, about 50 minutes. Cut the peppers into strips or chunks and add to the stew. Season to taste with salt and cayenne pepper; garnish with parsley.

MASHED POTATOES

Cook the potatoes in a saucepan of boiling water until tender. Drain, saving ⅓ cup (80 ml) of the cooking liquid. Mash the potatoes. Add the milk, sour cream, and, if necessary, a little of the cooking liquid. Season to taste with salt.

Serve the stew on top of a bed of mashed potatoes.

LEFTOVERS?
THE STEW CAN BE REHEATED THE FOLLOWING DAY.

Parsley is rich in healthful nutrients and volatile oils that can activate our own antioxidants to help protect against cancer. It appears that parsley may help protect the body from the harmful effects of cigarette smoke. Add fresh parsley to salads, soups, stir-fries, and casseroles to bolster both flavor and nutritional value.

SALAD WRAPS WITH SLICED PORK AND PURÉED SUNCHOKES

Large, sturdy lettuce leaves are perfect for wraps. Here, pork strips and sunchokes make a tasty filling.

1 large head romaine lettuce

VINAIGRETTE

1 tablespoon coarse mustard

1 teaspoon honey

Juice of ½ organic lemon

2 tablespoons apple cider vinegar

¼ cup (60 ml) olive oil

½ apple, cored and diced

2 tablespoons finely chopped
  red onion

MASHED SUNCHOKES

1 pound (500 g) unpeeled
  sunchokes

2 tablespoons canola oil

Salt and freshly ground pepper

Fresh organic lemon juice

4 boneless pork chops
  (1¼ lb/625 g total)

Salt and freshly ground pepper

2 tablespoons canola oil

2 onions, cut into wedges

3–4 garlic cloves, minced

4 radishes

Watercress sprigs

Tear off 8 large outer lettuce leaves for the wraps. Cut the romaine heart into strips.

VINAIGRETTE

In a bowl, whisk the mustard, honey, and lemon juice together and then whisk in the vinegar, followed by the olive oil. Fold in the diced apple, red onion, and lettuce strips.

MASHED SUNCHOKES

Cut the sunchokes into chunks. Heat the canola oil in a saucepan and cook the sunchokes until lightly browned. Add water to come halfway up the sides of the sunchokes. Bring to a boil, reduce to a simmer, cover, and cook the sunchokes until tender. Mash them with a fork. Season with salt, pepper, and a few drops of lemon juice.

Preheat the oven to 350°F (180°C).

Sprinkle the chops with salt and pepper. In an ovenproof frying pan, heat the canola oil and brown the chops on both sides. Add the onion wedges and garlic cloves to the pan. Transfer to the oven and bake for 5–6 minutes. Using tongs, transfer the meat to a cutting board and return the onions and garlic to the oven. Let the meat cool for 4–5 minutes, then cut it into strips. Let the onions bake until tender. Return the meat slices to the pan to heat through. Cut the radishes into thin slices. Put them into ice cold water so they will stay crisp until serving.

SERVING

Fill the lettuce leaves with the watercress, meat strips, and baked onions. Serve the mashed sunchokes, radish slices, and vinaigrette alongside the wraps.

Most people add black pepper to their food to improve the flavor, but pepper also contributes to our health in several ways. Pepper stimulates the taste buds, sending signals to the stomach to increase the production of stomach acids. It helps with the absorption of nutrients from protein-rich food. In addition, the element piperidine in freshly ground pepper actually increases the absorption of vitamins, minerals, and plant fiber from food. Make sure your peppermill is always full and ready for guests around the table.

CHARCUTERIE DINNER

For this meal, you can combine leftover cured meats with cold cuts from the deli. With good sides, this makes a tasty and flavorful dinner. I am sure you already have your own way of making scrambled eggs, but I want to show you my way, using a double boiler. Have cornichons, pickled beets, flatbread (homemade, page 184), and crispbread on hand for serving.

1¼ pounds (625 g) assorted cold cuts

SOUR CREAM DRESSING
⅓ cup (80 ml) sour cream

2 tablespoons heavy cream

Salt and freshly ground pepper

Fresh organic lemon juice

Red onion slices

Minced fresh chives

GREEN SALAD WITH NUT VINAIGRETTE
¾ cup (100 g) hazelnuts

1 tablespoon honey

2 tablespoons apple cider vinegar

3 tablespoons olive oil

3 cups (90 g) mixed lettuces

SCRAMBLED EGGS
6 eggs, beaten

3 tablespoons heavy cream

Salt and cayenne pepper

2 tablespoons clarified butter

Minced fresh chives

Arrange the cold cuts on a platter or cutting board.

SOUR CREAM DRESSING
In a bowl, whisk the sour cream and heavy cream. Season to taste with salt, pepper, and a little lemon juice. Transfer to a serving bowl. Lay the onion slices on top and sprinkle with chives.

Preheat the oven to 325°F (160°C).

SALAD WITH NUT VINAIGRETTE
Toast the hazelnuts on a rimmed baking sheet in the oven until they begin to color. Rub off the skins in a towel and then coarsely chop the nuts. In a bowl, whisk the honey, vinegar, and oil and then fold in the warm nuts. Toss with the lettuce just before serving.

SCRAMBLED EGGS
In a bowl, whisk the eggs with the cream and season with salt and cayenne pepper. Melt the butter in the top of a double boiler. Pour in the egg-cream mixture. Using a wooden spoon, stir the eggs up from the bottom. When the eggs are creamy, transfer to a serving dish. Garnish with chives.

LEFTOVERS?
EVERYTHING CAN GO INTO THE LUNCH BOX THE NEXT DAY.

PORK CHOPS WITH GRAPEFRUIT AND MASHED PEAS

Here is a complete and tasty meal. The tartness of grapefruit is balanced with the sweet flavor of pork. The chops can be fried on the stove top or grilled.

GRAPEFRUIT VINAIGRETTE

1 grapefruit

2 tablespoons capers

2 tablespoons minced fresh chives

⅓ cup (80 ml) olive oil

Salt and freshly ground pepper

Fresh organic lemon juice

MASHED PEAS

10 ounces (315 g) frozen green peas

⅓ cup (80 ml) olive oil

¼ cup (60 g) butter

Salt and freshly ground pepper

RAW VEGGIE SALAD

1 large red beet

1 large yellow beet

2 cups (60 g) lightly packed baby spinach

¼ cup (60 ml) olive oil

Salt and freshly ground pepper

Fresh organic lemon juice

1¾ pounds (875 g) pork chops

Salt and freshly ground pepper

Watercress sprigs

GRAPEFRUIT VINAIGRETTE

Peel the grapefruit with a sharp knife and remove the bitter white pith. Segment the grapefruit by cutting between the membranes. Cut into smaller chunks. In a bowl, combine the capers, chives, and oil. Season to taste with salt, pepper, and lemon juice. Add the grapefruit.

MASHED PEAS

Simmer the frozen peas in a saucepan of lightly salted boiling water for 4–5 minutes. Drain, saving ⅔ cup (160 ml) cooking water. Mash the peas with the olive oil and butter. Thin to the desired thickness with the cooking water. Season to taste with salt and pepper. Set aside and keep warm.

RAW VEGGIE SALAD

Peel the beets and sliver them with a cheese slicer. In a bowl, toss them with the spinach and olive oil. Season to taste with salt, pepper, and a few drops of lemon juice.

PORK CHOPS

In a frying pan over medium-high heat, cook the pork chops for 6–7 minutes on each side. Season with salt and pepper. Top each pork chop with vinaigrette. Garnish with watercress.

The olive oil in the mashed peas adds a spicy flavor. Use whatever cold-pressed olive oil you like.

SWEET-AND-SOUR
BAKED CHICKEN QUARTERS

I like the combination of flavors in sweet-and-sour chicken.
In this dish, salty sausage and sweet apricots do wonders.

2 red onions

8 shallots

1 whole head garlic

¼ cup (60 ml) olive oil

Salt and freshly ground pepper

Fresh organic lemon juice

4 chicken quarters
  (legs with thighs)

SALAD

2 heads romaine lettuce

4 ounces (125 g) Spanish (smoked)
  chorizo sausages, thinly sliced

2 ounces (60 g) blanched almonds

⅓ cup (60 g) dried organic
  apricots, coarsely chopped

⅓ cup (80 m) olive oil

MAYONNAISE

1 egg yolk

1 teaspoon mustard

1¼ cups (310 ml) olive oil

Grated zest and juice of
  ½ organic lemon

Salt

Chopped fresh parsley

Preheat the oven to 400°F (200°C).

Coarsely chop the onions and shallots. Separate the garlic into unpeeled cloves. In a baking dish, combine the onions, shallots, and garlic with the oil. Season with salt, pepper, and lemon juice. Toss to coat and place the chicken on top. Bake for 30 minutes, or until the chicken is golden and crisp.

SALAD

Cut the romaine in half lengthwise and then crosswise into large pieces. Fry the chorizo slices until golden in a dry frying pan. Stir in the almonds, apricots, and olive oil. Strew over the lettuce.

MAYONNAISE

In a bowl, whisk the egg yolk and mustard with the olive oil. Stir in the lemon zest and juice. Season to taste with salt. Spoon dollops of the mayonnaise on the lettuce.

Garnish the chicken with parsley and serve with the salad alongside.

LEFTOVERS?

PICK THE CHICKEN MEAT OFF THE BONES AND COOK IN CREAM WITH THE ONIONS. SERVE WITH THE REMAINING SALAD.

Without onions, the world would be a duller place. This flavorful and exceptional vegetable comes in all sorts of varieties. Yellow onions are the most common and work well in dishes that need some sweetness. Red onions, on the other hand, have a sharper flavor and are excellent in dishes that need more bite; they are also good in raw dishes.

CHAPTER 3

SMALL DISHES

PERHAPS YOU THINK THAT YOU CAN DO WITHOUT IT, BUT MOST PEOPLE HAVE AN IRRESISTIBLE URGE FOR SOMETHING TASTY IN THE HOURS BEFORE DINNER. YOU NEED SOMETHING TO SNACK ON WHEN YOUR STOMACH BEGINS TO GROWL. WE ALL BECOME A LITTLE PECKISH. THE TRICK IS TO MAKE HEALTHFUL SNACKS AND PREDINNER APPETIZERS. RESTRICT YOURSELF TO VEGETABLES AND TOPPINGS THAT ALSO MAKE YOUR BODY HAPPY. YOU CAN GO FOR HEALTHY FAST FOOD SUCH AS CURED HAM OR A SALAD. YOU WILL BE WELL SATISFIED WITH SIMPLE PROTEINS AND LOTS OF GOOD FLAVOR.

FLATBREAD WITH HAM AND SOUR CREAM SAUCE

Flatbread with cured meat, onion, and sour cream is a satisfying snack to serve year-round. For homemade flatbread, see page 184. You can substitute roast lamb for the ham.

1 onion, finely chopped

3 tablespoons sour cream

Salt

Fresh organic lemon juice

1 tablespoon grated horseradish

8 flatbreads

8 slices cured ham, such as prosciutto or serrano ham

Mâche and frisée or mixed baby lettuces

In a bowl, combine the onion and sour cream and season to taste with salt and lemon juice. Stir in the horseradish. Spread on pieces of flatbread. Top with the ham slices and a handful of mâche.

Flatbread can be served with almost anything. You can find all sorts of flatbreads in the market, but making it yourself is easier than you might think. If you have the time, make a large amount of dough and cook a big batch (see page 184). The advantage of cooking flatbread yourself is that you can use more nutritious flour and avoid unnecessary additives. Flatbread will stay crisp and tasty for quite a while.

CRUDITÉS WITH HERRING CREAM

The best thing about this snack is the successful interplay between the vegetables and the dip.

2 ounces (60 g) smoked herring fillets
or smoked mackerel

⅔ cup (170 ml) sour cream

¼ cup (60 ml) cream cheese

Freshly ground pepper / Fresh organic lemon juice

Assortment of crudités, such as carrot and
celery sticks, endive leaves, radishes,
and broccoli, washed and sliced as needed

In a blender, process the herring, sour cream, and cream cheese until smooth. Season with salt and pepper. Serve the vegetables alongside the herring cream for dipping.

CHEESE SANDWICHES

This dish will help you use up stale bread.

8 slices stale rustic-style bread, thinly sliced

8 slices cooked ham

8 slices Gruyère or another firm cheese

2 tablespoons canola oil / 3 tablespoons sour cream

1 tablespoon Dijon mustard / Salt and ground pepper

Fresh organic lemon juice

2 cups lightly packed baby lettuces

Lay 4 slices of bread on a cutting board. Top each with ham and cheese and then another slice of bread. In a frying pan, heat the oil over medium heat and sauté the sandwiches until golden on each side and the cheese has melted. In a bowl, mix the sour cream and mustard and season to taste with salt, pepper, and lemon juice. Divide the dressing and the lettuce over the sandwiches.

CUCUMBER AND AVOCADO SOUP

Cucumber and avocado? Did you hear that right? Give it a chance. This soup is a flavor bomb full of vitamins, minerals, and beneficial fatty acids.

2 unpeeled cucumbers
1 avocado, peeled, pitted, and chopped
¾ cup (180 ml) plain Greek yogurt
¾ cup (180 ml) whole milk
1 garlic clove, chopped
2 teaspoons grated fresh ginger
Juice of ½ organic lemon / Fresh mint leaves

In a food processor, process all the ingredients except the mint until smooth. Serve immediately in small soup bowls and garnished with mint leaves.

HAM AND PARMESAN OMELET

An omelet elevates eggs to a higher level. It's quick to make and rich in vitamins and flavor.

3 eggs / 2 tablespoons heavy cream
Salt and cayenne pepper / 1 tablespoon canola oil
3 thin slices ham / Grated Parmesan cheese
Garden cress or sprouts

In a bowl, whisk the eggs with the cream. Season with salt and cayenne pepper. In a frying pan, heat the oil over low heat, pour in the eggs and cook until firm on the bottom, lifting the edges of the eggs to let the liquid flow into the pan. Place the ham on top, sprinkle with the Parmesan, and garnish with cress.

STEAK SANDWICHES

I'll never forget my first steak sandwich, which I ate in the United States almost twenty years ago. The meat was tender and perfectly grilled. I just have to close my eyes now to remember the harmony between the meat, the mayonnaise, and the crispy toasted bread.

8 ounces (250 g) sirloin steak

Salt and freshly ground pepper

2 tablespoons canola oil

MAYONNAISE

1 egg yolk

1 tablespoon apple cider vinegar

1 tablespoon mustard

1¼ cups (310 ml) canola or olive oil

Salt and cayenne pepper

Fresh organic lemon juice

2 rustic-style baguettes

1 tablespoon butter

3 ounces (90 g) chanterelles or
other mushrooms, sliced

8 small cornichons,
or 3 tablespoons sliced pickles

2 cups lightly packed mixed baby
lettuce

2 ounces (60 g) Parmesan cheese,
sliced

2 shallots, sliced

Preheat the oven to 350°F (180°C).

Sprinkle the meat with salt and pepper. In a frying pan, heat the oil and brown the meat on both sides. Transfer to the oven and cook for 10–15 minutes, or to 140°F (60°C) for medium rare and 155°F (68°C) for medium. Let the meat cool for 10 minutes before slicing it.

MAYONNAISE

Whisk the egg yolk, vinegar, and mustard in a bowl. Continue whisking as you drizzle in the oil until the consistency is airy and thoroughly blended. Season with salt, cayenne pepper, and a few drops of lemon juice.

Halve each baguette horizontally and scoop out the centers. Melt the butter in a frying pan and crumble in the scooped bread. Add the mushrooms and cook until golden and crisp. Slice the cornichons and mix them with the lettuce, Parmesan, and shallots. Fill the baguette "boats" with the meat and vegetables and top with dollops of mayonnaise.

You can use whatever type of meat
you like in this dish, including leftover
roast beef, turkey, chicken, or lamb.

TOASTED GOAT CHEESE

With its golden crust and runny interior, toasted goat cheese
is a pure burst of flavor. It's a perfect between-meals snack.

14-ounces (440 g) fresh white goat cheese

½ cup (60 g) walnuts

1 tablespoon honey

1 tablespoon fresh organic lemon juice

2 tablespoons olive oil

Mâche or mixed baby lettuces

Preheat the oven to 400°F (200°C).

Cut the cheese into 4 disks. Heat a dry frying pan over medium heat and toast them until golden on one side. Toast the walnuts in a pie pan in the oven for 7–8 minutes.

In a bowl, combine the honey, lemon juice, and oil. Add the nuts and toss to coat. Stir in the mâche and serve with the cheese.

Nuts in salad, nuts in vinaigrette, nuts in cakes and dinner dishes: Yes, please. Nuts have beneficial fats, fiber, phytonutrients, vitamins, and minerals. On top of all that, they taste great. Nuts are best kept in air-tight containers in a cool, dark place. The fatty acids will become harsh and disintegrate over time, so buy fresh nuts and enjoy them!

COLD TOMATO SOUP

This soup, reminiscent of a Bloody Mary cocktail or gazpacho, is a powerhouse of nutrition because none of its beneficial elements have been destroyed by heat.

1 cucumber, chopped

4 roasted peppers (from a jar), chopped

1 red chile, chopped

1 pound (500 g) fresh tomatoes, chopped

1¼ cups (310 ml) tomato juice

½ cup (250 ml) olive oil

Juice of 1 organic lemon

2 tablespoons Worcestershire sauce

Salt and freshly ground pepper

1 celery stalk, cut into 4 sticks

Fresh cilantro leaves

Ice cubes (optional)

In a food processor, process the cucumber, peppers, chile, and tomatoes with the tomato juice, olive oil, lemon juice, and Worcestershire sauce until smooth. Season to taste with salt and pepper. Serve in soup bowls with celery sticks, cilantro leaves, and ice cubes, if you like.

The combination of olive oil and tomatoes makes this dish extra healthy. The fat in the oil facilitates the absorption of lycopene in the tomatoes. Try serving tomato slices drizzled with olive oil for any meal.

CREAMED TROUT ON FLATBREAD

Creamed fish and crisp flatbread are a flavorful and saisfying combination.

FLATBREAD

⅓ cup (80 ml) lukewarm water

1 tablespoon honey

½ teaspoon salt

½ cup (60 g) white spelt flour

¾ cup (90 g) light rye flour

CREAMED TROUT

7 ounces (220 g) cooked trout

½ cup (125 g) cream cheese

2 tablespoons sour cream

1 tablespoon plain Greek yogurt

Salt and freshly ground pepper

Fresh organic lemon juice

Garden cress or sprouts

FLATBREAD

In a bowl, combine all the ingredients and stir until the dough holds together well. Divide into pieces. On a floured work surface, roll out each piece until very thin. In a warm, dry frying pan, cook the bread for 1½ minutes on each side. Stack the bread on a kitchen towel.

CREAMED TROUT

In a food processor or a bowl, combine all the ingredients and pulse or stir until smooth. Spread over the flatbread and garnish with cress.

Watercress has a peppery, spicy flavor. Its relative, garden cress, can be grown in a few days. Line a container 2-inches (1-cm) deep with a paper towel, spray with water to saturate, sprinkle on the seeds, and cover with plastic wrap. Place in a window indoors. Enjoy watching it grow day by day. When it's green, it's ready to eat. Use it to garnish casseroles and salads.

BREAD SALAD

This is a version of Italian panzanella. It's fast to make and
offers a fine balance of flavors and textures.

8 slices prosciutto or serrano ham

4 slices bread

3 tablespoons olive oil

2 garlic cloves, minced

1 avocado, peeled and pitted

8 cornichons

2 shallots, sliced

1 teaspoon honey

1 tablespoon apple cider vinegar

Olive oil

Mâche or baby lettuces

½ cup (60 g) grated Parmesan
cheese

Preheat the oven to 350°F (180°C).

Spread the prosciutto slices on a baking sheet lined with parchment paper. Bake until crisp, 8–10 minutes. Drain on paper towels. Cut the bread into large cubes. In a bowl, combine the olive oil and garlic. Add the bread and toss to coat. In a frying pan, sauté the bread until golden; empty into a salad bowl. Cut the avocado and cornichons into bite-sized pieces and add to the bread mixture along with the shallots

In a bowl, whisk together the honey, vinegar, and olive oil to make a dressing. Add to the bread mixture along with the mâche and toss to coat. Break the crisp prosciutto into pieces over the salad, then sprinkle with Parmesan.

Prosciutto and serrano ham are cured meats that
have been salted and dried until the meat acquires a
concentrated flavor. If you add it to a dish, limit the salt for
the rest of the dish. If you grate Parmesan cheese over a
dish, you'll increase the amount of calcium considerably.

MUSHROOM STEW WITH POACHED EGGS

This flavorful dish is both rich and comforting.

2 tablespoons butter

10½ ounces (310 g) cremini or chanterelle mushrooms

2 shallots, minced

½ garlic clove, chopped

⅓ cup (80 ml) heavy cream

Salt and freshly ground pepper

Fresh organic lemon juice

POACHED EGGS
4 eggs

⅓ cup (80 ml) vinegar

Salt

Chopped fresh parsley leaves

MUSHROOM STEW

Melt the butter in a frying pan over medium heat and sauté the mushrooms, shallots, and garlic until they take on a deep color. Stir in the cream and cook for 3–5 minutes. Season to taste with salt, pepper, and lemon juice. Cover and keep warm.

POACHED EGGS

Crack each egg into a separate cup. Bring water to a boil in a deep, wide pan. Stir in the vinegar and salt. Remove the pan from the heat. While using a ladle to keep the water swirling, pour one egg into the water and cook until the white is opaque, 2–3 minutes. Using a slotted spoon, transfer the egg to a plate and repeat to cook the remaining eggs.

Serve each portion of the mushroom stew in a deep dish, top with a poached egg, and garnish with parsley.

Vinegar is a blend of acetic acid and water. The most highly regarded vinegars for cooking are made with wine. Good apple cider can also be used to make vinegar, and that is my favorite. It's fruity but neutral and can be used in almost all dishes calling for vinegar. One good bonus of weak acids, such as vinegar, as well as lemon and lime juices, is that they are transformed into alkaline in the body and help you maintain a good pH balance, especially if you eat much meat, which produces strong acids (urea) in the body. You can also drink a little water flavored with vinegar, lemon, or lime.

HAM ROLLS WITH HAZELNUT VINAIGRETTE

A healthy and savory snack.

½ cup (60 g) hazelnuts

1 tablespoon honey

1 tablespoon apple cider vinegar

3 tablespoons olive oil

1 tablespoon minced fresh chives

2 cups (60 g) lightly packed mâche or baby lettuces

8 slices cured ham, such as prosciutto or serrano

Toast the hazelnuts in a dry frying pan on the stove top or in a pie pan in a preheated 325°F (165°C). Rub them in a towel to remove the skins, then coarsely chop the nuts.

In a bowl, whisk the honey, vinegar, and oil together and then stir in the nuts and chives. In a bowl, dress the lettuce with the vinaigrette. Spread the ham slices on a platter. Fill each with one-eighth of the dressed lettuce and roll up.

For those who are concerned about salt, it is important to note that about 70 percent of the salt we consume comes from processed food. If processed food is part of your diet, taste a dish before adding salt. In the kitchen, choose mineral-rich sea salt rather than table salt.

ENERGY BARS

Make sure to keep these energy bars on hand. That way, you'll always
have some when hunger strikes and you need a good snack.

½ cup (90 g) oatmeal

⅓ cup (60 g) raisins

¾ cup (90 g) almonds,
    coarsely chopped

½ cup (60 g) sunflower seeds

⅓ cup (60 g) dried organic
    apricots, coarsely chopped

1 egg yolk

⅓ cup (80 ml) honey

Grated zest of 2 organic lemons

⅓ cup (90 g) butter, melted

Preheat the oven to 350°F (180°C).

In a bowl, mix all the ingredients together. Empty the mixture onto a
work surface lined with parchment paper and roll out ¾ inch (2 cm) thick.
Transfer the slab and the parchment paper to a baking sheet. Bake until
dry, 20–25 minutes. Transfer to a wire rack to cool.

Cut the bars after they have cooled. If the bars aren't crisp, dry them in a
preheated oven for a few more minutes.

All kinds of nuts can be toasted until golden and crisp
in the oven, but they don't tolerate a high temperature;
their nutritional value can be destroyed if the heat is too
high. Toasting nuts concentrates the flavor and produces
a crunchy consistency. If you pour a little maple syrup
on nuts before toasting them, a crisp, sweet glaze will
transform them into a wonderful treat.

SMOKED TROUT AND AVOCADO ON CRISPBREAD

You couldn't ask for a tastier and easier-to-make fish salad.

8 ounces (250 g) smoked trout

1 avocado, peeled and pitted

1 tablespoon fresh organic
   lemon juice

2 tablespoons sour cream

3 tablespoons olive oil

Salt and freshly ground pepper

8 crispbreads or flatbreads
   (for homemade flatbread,
   see page 184)

Fresh cilantro leaves

Cut the trout into small pieces. Chop the avocado. In a bowl, combine the avocado, lemon juice, sour cream, and oil and mash coarsely with a fork. Fold in the trout pieces and season to taste with salt and pepper. Spread the mixture on crispbread or flatbread. Garnish with cilantro.

Coriander is both a spice and herb; fresh coriander is called cilantro, commonly used in Asian and Mexican cooking, and the dried seeds are used whole and ground as a spice in European and Middle Eastern cuisines. It's best to buy whole seeds and grind them yourself in a mortar or spice grinder so you get the richest flavor and most nutrients. Coriander can strengthen insulin production, help resist inflammation, and maintain a better fat-acid balance in the blood.

BAKED EGGS WITH MUSHROOMS AND SPINACH

Luckily, there are innumerable ways to cook eggs. In this recipe,
egg yolks add a delicious, creamy consistency to the mushrooms.

¼ cup (60 ml) canola oil

3 ounces (90 g) cremini or mixed
  mushrooms

1 shallot, sliced

1½ cups (45 g) lightly packed
  baby spinach

Salt and freshly ground pepper

2 tablespoons sour cream

8 eggs

Garden cress or sprouts

Preheat the oven to 350°F (180°C).

In a frying pan, heat the oil and sauté the mushrooms and shallot until golden. Stir in the spinach. Season to taste with salt and pepper. Divide among 4 individual gratin dishes. Top each with ½ tablespoon sour cream. Make two depressions in each spinach mixture and crack one egg into each depression. Bake in the oven for 8–10 minutes. Garnish each with garden cress to serve.

> Spinach is available year-round, both in bunches
> of mature leaves and bags of baby spinach.
> Either raw or cooked, it can be used for almost
> anything. Lay it under a topping on bread, mix
> a little into a tomato sauce, and add to green drinks.
> The fresher it is, the healthier it will be.

CHAPTER 4

WEEKEND MEALS

THERE SHOULD BE A DIFFERENCE BETWEEN FOOD SERVED ON
WEEKDAYS AND ON THE WEEKEND. THE WEEKEND IS THE
TIME FOR DINNER PARTIES AND CREATIVE COOKING,
WITH SPECIAL INGREDIENTS AND MORE AMBITIOUS RECIPES.
BUT IT'S ALSO THE TIME FOR LARGE, CASUAL GATHERINGS,
WHEN EVERYONE CAN COME TOGETHER WITH CHILDISH
DELIGHT OVER HOMEMADE TACOS OR THE HOUSE PIZZAS.
MANY WEEKEND MEALS CAN BE COOKED AS A JOINT ACTIVITY
WITH BOTH ADULTS AND CHILDREN. THE RESULTS WILL BE FESTIVE,
EVEN IF YOU PICKED UP THE INGREDIENTS AT THE CORNER STORE.

MUSSELS WITH GREEN CURRY SOUP AND LEFSE

Accompany this curried soup with lefse, the Norwegian version of naan,
a flatbread made here with yogurt and spelt flour.

LEFSE (MAKES 12)
1 tablespoon active dry yeast
(about 1½ packages)

⅓ cup (80 ml) half-and-half

1 cup (250 ml) plain Greek yogurt

1 teaspoon baking powder

3½ cups (425 g) white spelt flour

1 tablespoon honey

1 teaspoon salt

2 tablespoons olive oil

CURRY SOUP
2 garlic cloves, minced

2 shallots, minced

2 stalks lemongrass, white part
only, peeled

½ cup (80 g) minced fresh ginger

½ red chile, seeded and minced

Canola oil

1 tablespoon green curry paste

⅓ cup (80 ml) water

Juice of 3 limes

3 kaffir lime leaves, or zest strips
of 3 organic limes

2 cans coconut milk
(14 oz/420 ml each)

2 pounds (1 kg) mussels, rinsed

Fresh cilantro leaves

3 limes, cut into wedges

LEFSE
In a bowl, combine the yeast, half-and-half, and yogurt. Stir to blend. Sift the baking powder and flour into another bowl and then stir in the yeast mixture. Stir in the honey, salt, and oil until smooth. Cover the bowl with a damp cloth or plastic wrap and let the dough rest for 30 minutes. Divide the dough into 12 pieces. On a floured work surface, roll each piece until thin and then cook in a dry frying pan over medium heat until puffy and flecked with brown.

CURRY SOUP
In a frying pan, sauté the garlic, shallots, lemongrass, ginger, and chile in canola oil. Stir in the curry paste, then the water, lime juice, lime leaves, and coconut milk. Simmer for 30 minutes. Discard the lime leaves.

Cook the mussels in a cast-iron frying pan on the stove top until they open. Divide the mussels among serving bowls. Pour the soup over the mussels. Garnish with cilantro. Serve with lime wedges and warm lefse.

LEFTOVERS?
MIX THE MUSSELS WITH WHOLE-GRAIN PASTA AND ADD THE SAUCE FOR A TASTY LUNCH.

It's worth repeating that for safety's sake, if you're harvesting wild mussels, be sure to look for posted warnings at the beach and check online to make sure no poisonous algae is blooming along your stretch of coastline. Otherwise, buy farmed mussels at the fish counter

SALT-BAKED PLAICE WITH CREAMY CABBAGE AND WHITE BEANS

Salt-baked fish is especially moist. Here, it's served with hollandaise sauce for a party.

1 whole fish (4 lb/2 kg), such as plaice, snapper, or sea bass

Kosher salt for cooking

HOLLANDAISE SAUCE

1¼ cups (310 ml) dry white wine

2 shallots, minced

1 bay leaf

5 black peppercorns

3 egg yolks

1 tablespoon heavy cream

1 cup (250 ml) clarified butter

¼ cup (60 ml) olive oil

Salt and cayenne pepper

Fresh organic lemon juice

¾ cup (150 g) dried white beans, soaked overnight

½ small cabbage, cored

10 kale leaves

TOMATO SALAD

3–4 ripe tomatoes

1 cucumber

1 red onion, finely chopped

Fresh dill sprigs

Fresh organic lemon juice

3 tablespoons olive oil

Salt and freshly ground pepper

1 organic lemon

Preheat the oven to 350°F (180°C).

Cut the head and tail off the fish. Wash the fish and scrape off any protruding scales. Place the whole fish over a layer of salt in an ovenproof pan. Cover the top of the fish with another layer of salt. Bake the fish for 25–30 minutes. Transfer the fish to a platter and scrape off the skin. Remove any fine bones. Keep warm.

HOLLANDAISE SAUCE

In a saucepan, combine the wine, shallots, bay leaf, and peppercorns and cook until reduced to ¼ cup (125 ml). Strain and return the liquid to the pan. Whisk in the egg yolks and cream over very low heat until creamy. Gradually whisk in the butter. Season to taste with salt, cayenne pepper, and lemon juice.

Simmer the beans in a pot of salted water to cover until tender, 30–40 minutes. Cut the cabbage and kale into strips and cook in a saucepan of salted boiling water until tender, 3–4 minutes. Drain the cabbage and kale and add them and the beans to the sauce.

TOMATO SALAD

Cut the tomatoes and cucumber into chunks and place in a bowl. Add the red onion and sprinkle with dill. Drizzle with lemon juice and olive oil. Sprinkle with salt and pepper.

Cut the lemon into wedges and serve alongside the fish and the salad.

Hollandaise made from scratch and eaten in reasonable amounts contributes the nutritional benefits of spices, egg yolks, and butter. When you also blend in a healthy portion of vegetables, you can enjoy the sauce without a guilty conscience.

Don't throw away stale bread. You can use it in various ways: fry bread crumbs until crisp for salads or toast croutons for soup or salad. You can also make your own bread crumbs for breading, as in this recipe. The less food you throw away, the better for all of us!

CRAB CAKES WITH LEMON MAYONNAISE, CORN, AND GREEN SALAD

This dish is a treat for adults but is also child-friendly. Serve the meal on paper plates and let the children get messy. Don't forget that small children try more foods when they feed themselves. And the dishes will be done in no time.

CRAB CAKES

6 ounces (185 g) white-fleshed fish fillet, such as pollock or snapper, chopped

Pinch of salt

1 egg

⅓ cup (80 ml) whole milk

6 ounces (185 g) fresh or vacuum-packed crabmeat

1 bunch green onions, trimmed and thinly sliced

½ chile, seeded and minced

1½ cups (200 g) dried bread crumbs for breading

2 tablespoons butter

LEMON MAYONNAISE

1 egg yolk

1 tablespoon mustard

Grated zest of 1 organic lemon

1 tablespoon apple cider vinegar

1¼ cups (310 ml) canola or olive oil

Salt and cayenne pepper

Fresh organic lemon juice

2 ears of corn, husked

10 ounces (315 g) mixed salad greens

2 avocados, peeled and pitted

Watercress sprigs

CRAB CAKES

Grind the fish with the salt in a food processor. Blend in the egg and milk. Empty the mixture into a bowl and stir in the crabmeat, green onions, and chile. Shape into balls with dampened hands or two spoons. Spread the bread crumbs on a platter. Roll the crab cakes in the crumbs so they are completely covered. Press the cakes to flatten slightly. In a frying pan, melt the butter and fry the crab cakes until golden, 2–3 minutes on each side. Set aside and keep warm.

LEMON MAYONNAISE

In a bowl, whisk the egg yolk with the mustard, lemon zest, and vinegar. Continue whisking as you slowly drizzle in the oil until the mixture is airy and thoroughly blended. Season with salt, cayenne pepper, and a few drops of lemon juice.

Broil the corn on the cob until lightly browned on all sides; cut into chunks. Arrange the salad greens on a platter. Slice the avocado and layer on top of the salad. Arrange the crab cakes and corn around the edges of the platter. Top the salad with dollops of the mayonnaise and garnish with watercress.

LEFTOVERS?

ANY LEFTOVER CRAB CAKES CAN BE SERVED ON BREAD AND TOPPED WITH MAYONNAISE THE NEXT DAY.

TURBOT WITH CREAMED VEGETABLES AND CRISPY ONIONS

This sought-after fish, turbot, gives you many fine reasons to cook it. You could also use other types of flatfish, such as sole. Make an extra batch of crispy onions, because the leftovers can be used in several other dishes during the week.

4 turbot or sole fillets (1¼ lb/625 g total), skinned

Salt and freshly ground pepper

2–3 tablespoons canola oil

3 garlic cloves, sliced

4 sprigs fresh thyme

Fresh organic lemon juice

BUTTER SAUCE

⅔ cup (160 ml) heavy cream

2 tablespoons white wine vinegar

10 tablespoons (155 g) cold butter

Salt and cayenne pepper

Fresh organic lemon juice

CREAMED VEGETABLES

1 pound (500 g) Yukon gold potatoes, peeled

1 cabbage, cored and cut into strips

1 bunch green asparagus, trimmed and cut into 2-inch (5-cm) pieces

1 bunch broccoli, cut into florets

Minced fresh chives

CRISPY ONIONS

1 onion

⅓ cup (80 ml) whole milk

¼ cup (30 g) fine spelt flour

1 tablespoon canola oil

Chopped fresh chives

Garden cress or sprouts

Sprinkle the fillets with salt and pepper. In a frying pan, heat the oil and fry the fish, skinned side down, until crisp. Remove from the heat. Add the garlic and thyme. Turn the fillets and let them sizzle for a few seconds in the heat. Transfer the fish to a plate. Return the pan to the heat and stir in the lemon juice. Pour the juices over the fish to serve. Set aside and keep warm.

BUTTER SAUCE

Combine the cream and vinegar in a saucepan and cook to reduce by one-third. Gradually whisk the butter into the sauce by the tablespoonful until melted. Remove from the heat and season to taste with salt, cayenne pepper, and lemon juice. Keep warm over lukewarm water.

CREAMED VEGETABLES

Cook the potatoes in a saucepan of salted boiling water until tender; drain and cut into large pieces. In another saucepan of salted boiling water, cook the cabbage, asparagus, and broccoli until tender; drain. Add the vegetables and potatoes to the butter sauce.

CRISPY ONIONS

Cut the onion into thin slices. Pour the milk into a saucepan and add the onion slices. Bring to a boil and cook for 3–4 minutes; drain, reserving the milk for a soup or a sauce. Dry the onion slices on paper towels and separate into rings. Toss the onion in the flour to coat evenly. Heat the oil in a frying pan and fry until crisp.

Garnish the creamed vegetables with chives and the fish with garden cress and serve with the crispy onions alongside.

LEFTOVERS?

USE THE LEFTOVERS TO MAKE A TEMPTING HASH.

When frying fish fillets without the skin, fry them first on the side that had the skin. The fat layer between the skin and fish meat yields an especially good crust and fish flavor.

SHELLFISH BONANZA

This salad features crayfish, scallops, oysters, and crab with toasted rye bread.
To top off the experience, make your own mayonnaise. It doesn't get any better than this!

4 sea scallops

2 tablespoons olive oil

Sea salt

1 tablespoon minced fresh chives

Juice of ½ organic lemon

2½ tablespoons minced fresh
   tarragon

2 pounds (1 kg) crayfish

¼ cup (125 g) butter,
   at room temperature

2 garlic cloves, minced

Salt and cayenne pepper

Fresh organic lemon juice

12 oysters

Rock salt for serving

2 limes

LEMON MAYONNAISE

1 egg yolk

1 tablespoon apple cider vinegar

1 tablespoon Dijon mustard

1¼ cups (310 ml) canola or olive oil

Grated zest of 1 organic lemon

Salt and cayenne pepper

Fresh organic lemon juice

7 ounces (220 g) fresh or
   vacuum-packed crabmeat

2 hearts of romaine lettuce

Canola oil

4–6 slices rye bread

Garden cress, sprouts,
   or edible flowers

Thinly slice the scallops crosswise. Arrange on a wide plate. Drizzle with the oil. Sprinkle with sea salt and chives. Squeeze lemon juice over scallops and sprinkle with 1 tablespoon of tarragon to serve.

Cut the crayfish in half lengthwise and remove the dark vein that runs through the tail meat. Place the crayfish in a baking dish. In a food processor, blend the butter, the remaining 1½ tablespoons of the tarragon, and garlic. Season with salt, cayenne pepper, and lemon juice. Spread the butter over the crayfish, and broil for 4–5 minutes.

Shuck the oysters and loosen the meat from the bottom shell. Spread salt over a plate and arrange the oysters on top in the half shell. Cut the limes into wedges and serve with the oysters.

LEMON MAYONNAISE
Remove the ingredients from the refrigerator 30 minutes before making, so that they're at room temperature. In a bowl, whisk the egg yolk with the vinegar, mustard, and lemon zest. Continue whisking as you slowly drizzle in the oil until the mixture is smooth, airy, and thoroughly blended. Season with salt, cayenne pepper, and lemon juice.

Pick over the crabmeat for cartilage. Tear the lettuce into pieces. In a frying pan, heat the oil and fry the rye bread until crisp and then tear into pieces. In a bowl, mix the crabmeat, lettuce leaves, rye bread, and 2–3 tablespoons lemon mayonnaise. Serve in a salad bowl and garnish with garden cress.

LEFTOVERS?
SHOULD YOU UNEXPECTEDLY HAVE SHELLFISH LEFT OVER, YOU CAN MAKE A PAELLA WITH WILD RICE FOR LUNCH THE NEXT DAY.

We can't say this often enough: Homemade mayonnaise is a tasty and easily made alternative. If you make a larger amount than you need right away, the mayonnaise can be stored in an airtight jar in the refrigerator.

It has been shown that there is a lot of wisdom in the old saying, "Eating herring makes you kind." In contrast to farm-raised fish, herring eat only natural seafood. For that reason, the fish meat abounds with beneficial fats that can improve your mood, concentration, and memory. What kind of herring should you choose? Herring is designated by its stage of development. Small herring are called sprats and kippers. Fat herring are another step of development, at 8–12 herring per 2 pounds (1 kg). These herring, which are not mature enough for breeding, are used for pickled herring. Large herring come to the Norwegian coast to mate. After mating, they are called spring herring. You can fry or cook these fish, or process them as cured or spiced herring.

MARINATED HERRING WITH SAUERKRAUT AND POTATO SALAD

The most neglected fast food on the Norwegian fresh food counters is salted herring, sour herring, and spiced herring. Give these healthy tidbits a chance for the weekend and get to know their potential as party food, even when it isn't Christmas.

POTATO SALAD

1¼ pounds (625 g) unpeeled Yukon gold potatoes

⅔ cup (160 ml) sour cream

Fresh organic lemon juice

Salt and freshly ground pepper

1 apple, cored and cut into julienne

2 tablespoons grated horseradish

Watercress leaves or garden cress

SAUERKRAUT

⅓ cup (80 ml) water

⅓ cup (80 ml) apple cider vinegar

1 tablespoon honey

1 small head cabbage, cored and cut into strips

4 eggs

Salt

Thinly sliced rustic-style bread

1¼ pounds (625 g) sour or spiced herring fillets

1 red onion, sliced

1 tablespoon minced fresh chives

POTATO SALAD

Cook the potatoes in a saucepan of salted simmering water until tender; drain. In a bowl, season the sour cream to taste with lemon juice, salt, and pepper. Dry the potatoes and slice them. Fold the potato slices and apple into the sour cream. Add the horseradish and toss to combine. Garnish with cress to serve.

SAUERKRAUT

Combine the water, vinegar, and honey in a nonreactive saucepan and bring to a boil. Add the cabbage, cover, cook for 20 minutes, and let cool. Boil the eggs in a saucepan for 6 minutes. Rinse them under cold running water, peel, cut them in half crosswise, and arrange them over the cooled cabbage. Season to taste with salt. Toast the bread and mix in with the sauerkraut just before serving.

Roll the herring fillets. Arrange them on a plate and garnish with red onion and chives.

LEFTOVERS?

IF YOU HAVE LEFTOVER HERRING, YOU CAN STUFF THIN POTATO PANCAKES (PAGE 110) OR THICK POTATO CAKES (PAGE 70) WITH IT TO ENJOY A HEALTHY WRAP.

HAKE WITH SMOKED HAM AND MASHED RUTABAGAS

Hake is a white cod harvested along the west coast of Norway year-round.
It is good for both baking and frying.

4 hake or other white-fleshed fish fillets (1¼ lb/625 g total)

4 slices smoked ham or bacon

2 tablespoons canola oil

MASHED RUTABAGAS

1¼ pounds (625 g) rutabagas

⅓ cup (80 ml) olive oil

SUNCHOKES AND LENTILS

½ cup (105 g) French green lentils

8 ounces (250 g) unpeeled sunchokes

2 tablespoons canola oil

2 tablespoons hazelnuts, coarsely chopped

1 tablespoon chopped dried organic apricot

2 tablespoons capers

1 teaspoon apple cider vinegar

3 tablespoons olive oil

Salt and freshly ground pepper

Fresh organic lemon juice

Fresh parsley leaves

Preheat the oven to 350°F (180°C).

Roll each fillet in a slice of smoked ham or bacon. In a frying pan, heat the oil and fry the rolls until the ham is golden all around. Transfer the rolls to a baking pan and bake for 2–3 minutes.

MASHED RUTABAGAS

Peel the rutabagas and cut into pieces. Cook in a saucepan of boiling salted water until tender; drain, reserving ⅓ cup (80 ml) of the cooking water. Mash the rutabagas in a bowl and stir in the olive oil. Thin with reserved cooking water if necessary.

SUNCHOKES AND LENTILS

Cook the lentils in a saucepan of salted simmering water until tender, about 20 minutes; drain and let cool. Cut sunchokes into chunks and cook in a saucepan of lightly salted boiling water until tender. In a frying pan, heat the oil and fry the sunchokes and nuts until golden. Blend in the lentils, apricot, and capers. Stir in the vinegar and oil. Season to taste with salt, pepper, and lemon juice. Garnish with parsley.

Arrange the fish rolls over the sunchoke mixture on a plate. Serve with the mashed rutabagas on the side.

The rutabaga has been called "Norway's orange." The name is totally applicable because both rutabagas and oranges are sources of beneficial C vitamins. Rutabagas, which are especially celebrated in Norway, Sweden, and Finland, are good raw as well as cooked in stews or fried. Norwegians who are overseas often struggle to find this root vegetable in markets. They are also known as "swedes."

PANFRIED COD WITH PICKLED VEGETABLES

Cod is an all-purpose fish. You can fry this fish with skin on in the pan, as in this recipe, or bake it in the oven, poach it, or marinate it raw.

PICKLED VEGETABLES

2 eggplants

2 yellow summer squash

5 ounces (155 g) roasted peppers (from a jar)

1 whole head garlic

2 red onions

2 yellow onions

Grated zest and juice of 1 organic lemon

2 tablespoons vinegar

Capers

¾ cup (180 ml) olive oil

1 can sardines in olive oil, drained

Fresh basil leaves for garnish

HERBED MAYONNAISE

1 egg yolk

1 tablespoon Dijon mustard

1 tablespoon apple cider vinegar

1¼ cups (310 ml) canola or olive oil

Salt and cayenne pepper

Fresh organic lemon juice

¼ cup mixed minced fresh herbs, such as basil, parsley, and chives

4 cod or halibut fillets (1¼ lb/625 g total), skin on

Toasted bread for serving

Salt and freshly ground pepper

1 tablespoon canola oil

10 sprigs fresh thyme

4 unpeeled garlic cloves

1 tablespoon butter

Preheat the oven to 350°F (180°C).

PICKLED VEGETABLES

Cut the vegetables into julienne. Divide the garlic into cloves. Cut the onions into wedges and put in a baking dish along with the vegetables and garlic. In a bowl, whisk together the lemon zest and juice, vinegar, capers, and oil. Stir into the vegetables. Cover the dish with aluminum foil and bake for 35–40 minutes. Uncover 5 minutes before the baking time is up. Top the vegetables with the sardines and basil for serving.

HERBED MAYONNAISE

In a bowl, whisk the egg yolk with the mustard and vinegar. Continue whisking as you slowly drizzle in the oil, until the consistency is airy and completely blended. Season with salt, cayenne pepper, and a few drops of lemon juice. Fold in the herbs.

Scrape any protruding scales from the fish skin. Rub salt and pepper on both sides of the fillets. In a frying pan, heat the oil and fry the fish, skin side down, until golden and crisp. Add the thyme and garlic cloves. Turn the fish and cook on the second side for 3 minutes. Stir in 1 tablespoon of butter and serve with the pickled vegetables, herbed mayonnaise, and toasted bread.

Grated lemon zest is a wonderful flavor enhancer.
Use organic lemons, if available.

WHEN CHILDREN HELP WITH THE COOKING, THE CHANCES ARE GREATER THAT THEY WILL TRY AND LIKE DIFFERENT FOODS.

IT'S FINE TO INDULGE IN **WEEKEND TREATS**, AS LONG AS YOU HAVE CONTROL OVER THE INGREDIENTS. **PREPARE A TACO PARTY WITH THE CHILDREN.**

CHICKEN TACOS

SPICE MIX
2 tablespoons ground cumin

½ teaspoon chili powder

2 tablespoons minced fresh cilantro

2 garlic cloves

2 tablespoons olive oil

Grated zest of ½ organic lemon

2 teaspoons salt

1¼ pounds (625 g) boneless
  chicken breasts, skin on

Canola oil

TORTILLAS (MAKES 8-12)
1½ cups (185 g) white spelt flour

1¼ cups (155 g) whole-grain
  spelt flour

2 tablespoons olive oil

1 cup (250 ml) lukewarm water

Salt

GUACAMOLE
3 avocados, peeled and pitted

1 red chile, seeded and minced

½ red onion, finely chopped

1 garlic clove, minced

3 tablespoons minced fresh cilantro

¼ cup (60 ml) olive oil

Salt and freshly ground pepper

Fresh organic lemon juice

TOMATO SALSA
4 cups (750 g) cherry tomatoes

½ red onion, finely chopped

1 garlic clove, minced

2 tablespoons olive oil

Fresh organic lemon juice

SOUR CREAM
¾ cup (180 ml) sour cream

2 tablespoons fresh lemon juice

2 tablespoons grated horseradish

Leaves from 1 head iceberg
  lettuce, torn

2 cups (250 g) shredded Cheddar
  or Muenster cheese

Preheat the oven to 350°F (180°C).

SPICE MIX
Blend all of the ingredients for the spice mix in a mortar or blender and crush or process until coarsely ground.

Spread the mixture under the chicken skin. In a frying pan, heat oil over medium heat and cook the chicken, skin side down, until the skin is brown and crisp. Turn the chicken over and transfer to a baking pan. Bake for 7–10 minutes, or until cooked through. Let the meat rest before slicing or cutting into strips.

TORTILLAS
In a bowl, mix all the ingredients for the tortillas to make a smooth dough. Cover with a kitchen towel and let rest for 15 minutes. Divide the dough equally on a floured work surface and roll out each piece into a thin round. Cook the tortillas in a dry frying pan over high heat. Stack the tortillas and cover with a kitchen towel.

GUACAMOLE
In a blender, combine all the ingredients for the guacamole, seasoning to taste with salt, pepper, and lemon juice, and blend until smooth.

TOMATO
In a bowl, combine all the ingredients for the tomato salsa, seasoning to taste with salt, pepper, and lemon juice, and pour into a serving bowl.

SOUR CREAM
In a bowl, stir all the ingredients for the sour cream together, seasoning to taste with salt and pepper.

Serve these components, along with the lettuce and cheese, as a taco buffet.

LEFTOVERS?
MAKE COLD TACO SALAD.

The advantages of cooking with garlic are endless. Yes, of course, it's healthy, and it has good flavor characteristics. I especially love to cook it with fish and meat. Split the garlic head in half, leaving the peel on, put it in the pan with the fish or meat, and the garlic will add extra flavor. You can also roast a whole garlic head on a bed of coarse salt in a preheated 350°F (180°C) oven until it is soft and sweet. The cooking time varies with the size of the garlic, but usually 15 minutes is enough. Oven-roasted garlic can be mashed right onto bread slices.

SPARERIBS WITH CREAMED CORN AND COLESLAW

The sides are all so good that they are guaranteed to complement the tasty ribs.
The extra marinade will keep for at least a week in the refrigerator—to use,
for example, for a spareribs party the following weekend.

MARINADE

½ cup (60 g) minced fresh ginger

1 red chile, seeded and minced

4 garlic cloves

1 stalk lemongrass, white part only, peeled

⅓ cup (80 ml) honey

1 tablespoon tomato paste

10 fennel seeds, ground

¾ cup (180 ml) apple juice or applesauce

4 cups (750 g) canned or boxed chopped tomatoes

⅓ cup (80 ml) apple cider vinegar

¼ cup (80 ml) soy sauce

4 pounds (2 kg) spareribs

1¼ pounds (625 g) large red potatoes

¼ cup (60 ml) olive oil

Salt and freshly ground pepper

1 tablespoon butter

2 cups (375 g) corn kernels

⅔ cup (160 ml) heavy cream

1 small head cabbage, cored

1 apple, cored and cut into julienne

⅓ cup (80 ml) sour cream

Fresh organic lemon juice

Horseradish

Watercress sprigs

Preheat the oven to 400°F (200°C).

MARINADE

Blend all the ingredients in a food processor until smooth. Pour into a wide pot.

Add the ribs to the marinade and add water to cover. Cook the meat until tender, about 1 hour. Transfer the ribs to a broiler pan.

Cut the potatoes in half lengthwise. Coat the potatoes in the oil in a bowl and sprinkle with salt and pepper. Spread the potatoes in a rimmed baking pan lined with parchment paper and bake on the lowest oven rack for 20 minutes. Place the broiler pan with the ribs on top of the baking pan with the potatoes. Bake for about 15 minutes, or until the meat is caramelized, golden, and crisp, and the juices have dripped down onto the potatoes.

In a saucepan, melt the butter and sauté the corn until golden. Pour in the cream and cook until the liquid is reduced. Season to taste with salt and pepper.

Cut the cabbage into thin strips and mix with the apple in a bowl. Stir in the sour cream and season to taste with lemon juice and salt. Grate horseradish over the slaw.

Garnish the spareribs with watercress sprigs and serve.

QUICK BEEF

As the name says, this meal is very quickly done as you stand over the stove.
The actual preparation consists mostly of buying and organizing.
If you can, bring marrow home from the butcher. It will increase the
nutritional value and enhance the flavor experience.

Rock salt for baking

8 small baking potatoes

⅔ cup (160 ml) sour cream

2 tablespoons finely chopped
onion

1 tablespoon minced fresh chives

Salt and freshly ground pepper

4 New York strip steaks
(1¼ lb/625 g total)

2 tablespoons canola oil

½ red onion, finely chopped

2 tablespoons capers

2 anchovies

2 sprigs fresh tarragon

1 tablespoon apple cider
or sherry vinegar

1 bunch broccolini or broccoli

12 ounces (375 g) Chinese long
beans (asparagus beans)

Handful of toasted almonds

Salt

1 organic lemon, cut into wedges

Preheat the oven to 400°F (200°C).

Cover the bottom of an ovenproof pan with rock salt. Slit lengthwise the top of each potato and nestle the potatoes in the salt. Bake for 40 minutes, or until tender. Squeeze the potato sides together to open the potatoes. Keep warm. In a bowl, mix the sour cream with the onion, chives, and a few grinds of pepper.

Salt and pepper the steaks. Heat the oil in an ovenproof frying pan and brown the steaks for 2–3 minutes on each side. Transfer the pan to the oven and bake the steaks for 2 minutes. Transfer the steaks to a platter and keep warm; reserve the frying pan.

Put the onion, capers, anchovies, and tarragon in the reserved frying pan. Pour in the vinegar. Cook over medium heat for a couple of minutes and keep warm.

Cook the broccolini in a saucepan of salted boiling water until tender, 2–3 minutes. Drain and arrange over the steaks.

Cook the long beans in salted water for 3–4 minutes, or until crisp-tender; drain and transfer to a serving bowl. (You can also steam the beans in a steamer to retain the nutrients, but it will take a little more time.) Mix the almonds with the long beans, season to taste with salt, and serve alongside the steaks.

Pour the dressing over the steaks to serve. Divide the sour cream among the potatoes. Serve the dishes with lemon wedges.

LEFTOVERS?

IF THERE IS TOO MUCH MEAT FOR THE DINNER, SERVE CHOPPED STEAK THE NEXT DAY.

The fattier the meat, the greater the flavor experience. Choose meat from grass-fed animals, both for the sake of the environment and for health considerations.

MOUSSAKA

This dish needs some preparation, but
once you've done all the various steps, you can rest
for a while before the guests are at the door.

1 pound (500 g) red potatoes

Salt

2 eggplants

3 tablespoons olive oil

MEAT SAUCE

2 tablespoons canola oil

1 pound (500 g) ground lamb or
   beef

2 onions, chopped

4 garlic cloves

2 red chiles, seeded and minced

10 sprigs fresh thyme

1 tablespoon minced fresh
   oregano,

14 ounces (440 g) fresh tomatoes,
   diced

WHITE SAUCE

2 tablespoons butter

¼ cup (30 g) white spelt flour

2½ cups (625 ml) whole milk

½ cup (125 g) grated Parmesan
   cheese

GREEN SALAD

1 head iceberg lettuce

1 tablespoon organic lemon juice

2 tablespoons oil

Cook the potatoes in a saucepan of salted boiling water until tender; drain and slice.

Preheat the oven to 400°F (200°C). Slice the eggplants crosswise. Sprinkle the slices with salt and let them "sweat" for 15 minutes. Dry off the salt and liquid. Spread the slices on a baking sheet lined with parchment paper. Drizzle them with olive oil. Bake for 15–20 minutes, or until tender.

Reduce the oven heat to 350°F (180°C).

MEAT SAUCE

In a frying pan, heat the oil over medium heat and fry the meat. Add the onions, garlic, chiles, and herbs. Sauté until the onion is translucent. Add the tomatoes and cook for 20 minutes.

WHITE SAUCE

Melt the butter in a saucepan and stir in the flour. Whisk in the milk and let the sauce cook for 10 minutes.

In an ovenproof pan, repeat these layers several times: meat sauce, potato slices, eggplant slices, and white sauce. The top layer should be white sauce. Top with Parmesan. Bake for 40 minutes.

GREEN SALAD

Tear the lettuce leaves into bite-sized pieces. Dress with lemon juice and olive oil. Serve with the moussaka.

LEFTOVERS?

BE HAPPY. MOUSSAKA IS AMONG THE GREAT DISHES THAT ARE EVEN BETTER THE NEXT DAY. JUST HEAT IT UP, MIX A FRESH SALAD, AND ENJOY.

HERBED CHICKEN WITH PICKLED ONIONS AND BRUSSELS SPROUTS

This dish is served with a pickled onion sauce, inspired by the sauces
often served with roasts and soup. The sauce takes good chicken to new heights!

6–8 sprigs fresh tarragon and
  parsley

1 whole chicken, about 4 pounds
  (2 kg)

Salt and freshly ground pepper

2 red onions

2 yellow onions

¾ cup (180 ml) water

¾ cup (180 ml) apple cider vinegar

2 tablespoons honey

1¼ cups (310 ml) heavy cream

BRUSSELS SPROUTS SALAD

⅔ cup (105 g) rye kernels,
  soaked overnight

10 ounces (315 g) brussels sprouts

Canola oil

1 shallot, minced

¼ cup (60 ml) olive oil

Salt and freshly ground pepper

Fresh organic lemon juice

¾ cup (90 g) walnuts

3 oranges, peeled and cut into
  segments

Preheat the oven to 350°F (180°C).

Stuff the herbs under the skin of the chicken breast. Sprinkle with salt
and pepper. Place the chicken in a nonreactive roasting pan.

Cut the onions into wedges and add them to the pan with the chicken.
Add the water, vinegar, and honey. Bake for 1 hour. Remove the chicken
and pour the pan juices into a saucepan. Add the cream. Cook to reduce.
In a blender or food processor, blend the sauce with the baked onions.
Strain and serve the sauce with the chicken.

BRUSSELS SPROUTS SALAD

Cook the rye kernels in a saucepan of lightly salted boiling water until
tender, 30–40 minutes. Drain. Trim the brussels sprouts, reserving the
outer leaves as a garnish. Cook the brussels sprouts in a saucepan of
salted water boiling water for 4–5 minutes, or until crisp-tender; drain.

In a saucepan, heat the canola oil and sauté the shallot until translucent.
Halve the cooked brussels sprouts and add them to the pan. Sauté until
they've taken on some color. Add the rye kernels. Stir in the olive oil and
season to taste with salt, pepper, and lemon juice. Toast the walnuts in
a dry frying pan. Toss into the salad with the orange segments, garnish
with the reserved brussels sprout leaves, and serve.

When buying whole chicken and chicken pieces, you can make a difference: Whenever possible, choose free-range chickens that were raised naturally and had a good quality of life. A little higher price per pound (kilo) will be compensated by beneficial nutrition for you and a better life for chickens.

HERBED PORK WITH OVEN-GRILLED FENNEL SALAD

This is a perennial favorite at our house. We share this festive secret with foodie friends.

1 piece center-cut boneless
   pork loin (2 lb/1 kg)

2 tablespoons coarse
   mustard

3 parsley sprigs

10 sage leaves

Salt and freshly ground
   pepper

Finely grated zest of
   1 organic lemon

BAKED FENNEL SALAD

4 fennel bulbs, trimmed
   (stalks and fronds reserved)

4 star anise

½ cup (250 ml) olive oil

½ cup (250 ml) dry
   white wine

Salt

FENNEL MAYONNAISE

1 egg yolk

1 tablespoon apple cider
   vinegar

1 tablespoon Dijon mustard

1¼ cups (310 ml) canola or
   light olive oil

Salt and cayenne pepper

Fresh organic lemon juice,
   to taste

Reserved fennel stalks

1 pound (500 g) small
   red potatoes

Olive oil

Preheat the oven to 375°F (190°C).

Butterfly the meat by making a lengthwise cut through the center, leaving the last inch or so attached, so you can open it like a book. Rub the cut side with mustard. Sprinkle the herbs, salt, pepper, and lemon zest over the meat. Fold the top of the meat over the bottom, sandwiching the herb mixture inside. Form the meat into a compact cylinder and secure closed by tightly tying about every 2-inches (5 cm) with cotton kitchen twine. Place the roast fat side up in an enameled cast-iron dutch oven or roasting pan just large enough to cover the meat. Add enough water to just cover the meat. Bake, partially covered, for about 2 hours, or until the internal temperature of the meat reaches 145°–150°F (63°–66°C). Add a bit more water to the bottom of the pan if the liquid dries out during baking. Remove the meat to a cutting board and keep warm. Let it rest for at least 15 minutes before slicing. Strain the pan juices into a small saucepan, spooning off the excess fat from the surface, and cook over medium-high heat to reduce to the consistency of *au jus*. Season with salt and pepper.

Lay out four 12-inch (31 cm) pieces of aluminum foil, shiny-side up. In a bowl, combine the whole fennel bulbs, star anise, oil, white wine, and salt. Toss to coat the fennel. Place 1 fennel bulb and ¼ of the oil-wine mixture on each piece of foil, topping each with a star anise. Bring up the sides of the foil to cover each bulb securely, and crimp the edges tightly to seal. Place the foil packets on a small baking sheet. Once the meat has been in the oven for 1 hour, add to the oven to bake along with the meat for 1 hour.

In a bowl, whisk together the egg yolk, vinegar, and mustard. Continue whisking and drizzle in the oil until the consistency is airy and thoroughly blended. Season with salt, cayenne pepper, and a few drops of lemon juice. Cut the fennel stalks into thin, 1-inch (2.5 cm) long matchstick-size pieces; fold into the mayonnaise.

Halve the potatoes and toss with the oil in a bowl. Place in a shallow baking dish and bake in the same oven until nicely browned and crispy on the edges, about 40 minutes

Trim excess fat from meat, if desired. Slice the meat and place the slices on warm plates with the baked potatoes. Drizzle the cooking juices over the meat.

Open the fennel packages, discard the star anise, and reserve the cooking juices. Cut the fennel bulbs into large bite-sized pieces and divide among the plates. Drizzle the reserved fennel cooking juices over each serving. Garnish with chopped fennel fronds. Pass the Fennel Mayonnaise at the table.

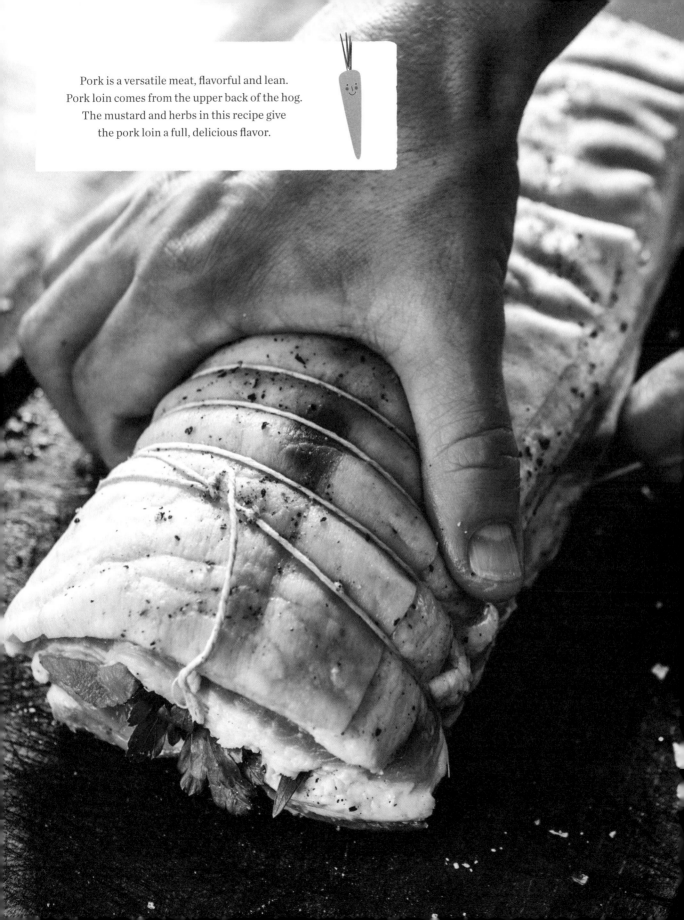

Pork is a versatile meat, flavorful and lean.
Pork loin comes from the upper back of the hog.
The mustard and herbs in this recipe give
the pork loin a full, delicious flavor.

SUNDAY TURKEY

Did you think turkey was just a seasonal phenomenon, only for Christmas and New Year's?
This big bird can be eaten all year and is a moist and healthy choice if the
bird was fed well, is prepared properly, and is served with complementary sides.

2 turkey breasts and 2 turkey legs,
  (6–8 lb/3–4 kg total)

Salt and freshly ground pepper

⅔ cup (160 ml) water

Olive oil

2 tablespoons canola oil

1 whole head garlic,
  halved crosswise

Small red potatoes

RED CABBAGE

14 ounces (440 g) red cabbage,
  cored

3 apples, cored

¼ cup (60 ml) honey

¼ cup (60 ml) apple cider vinegar

⅔ cup (160 ml) fresh orange juice

1 star anise

⅓ cup (80 ml) water

MUSHROOM STEW

8 ounces (250 g) chanterelles or
  other mushrooms

1–2 tablespoons canola oil

1 shallot, minced

¾ cup (180 ml) heavy cream

¼ cup (60 ml) whole milk

1 tablespoon sour cream

Salt and freshly ground pepper

Fresh organic lemon juice

Chopped fresh parsley

10 ounces (310 g) brussels sprouts

2 tablespoons canola oil

Preheat the oven to 350°F (180°C).

Season the turkey legs and breasts with salt and pepper. Put the thighs in a roasting pan and add the water. Drizzle with some olive oil and roast for 2½ hours, or until tender. In a frying pan, heat the canola oil and brown the turkey breasts and garlic. After about 60 minutes, add the turkey breasts to the roasting pan. After roasting, let the turkey rest for a while. Cut the thigh meat into slivers to add to the mushroom stew. Slice the turkey breasts.

In a bowl, toss the potatoes with some olive oil, salt, and pepper. Put on a baking pan and transfer to the oven at the same time as the turkey breasts.

RED CABBAGE

Cut the cabbage into fine strips. Cut the apples into wedges. Cook the honey in a soup pot until golden. Add the apple wedges and stir to coat. Add the vinegar, orange juice, star anise, and the cabbage. Pour in the water. Cover and cook for at least 40 minutes.

MUSHROOM STEW

Cut the mushrooms into large pieces. In a frying pan, heat the oil and fry the mushrooms and shallot until golden. Add the cream and milk and cook for 10–12 minutes. Stir in the sour cream. Season to taste with salt, pepper, and lemon juice. Add the reserved turkey thigh meat and the parsley.

BRUSSELS SPROUTS

Cook the brussels sprouts in a saucepan of lightly salted boiling water for 3–4 minutes. Drain. In a frying pan, heat the canola oil and fry the brussels sprouts just before serving.

Turkey is so closely associated with holidays that we often forget that it's available year-round. It makes delicious leftovers—any time of year!

All sorts of meat can be made into sausage,
but the stuffing mixture, or forcemeat,
has to be fatty so the sausages will be moist.
Heavy cream is both tasty and healthy
and will make the stuffing easy to prepare.

HOMEMADE SAUSAGES WITH MUSTARD CABBAGE

You can make sausage using a meat grinder and sausage stuffer or a stand mixer with a sausage attachment. You can also fill a piping bag with forcemeat and pull the casing onto it, then press the forcemeat through.

⅔ cup (100 g) pearl barley, soaked overnight

Salt and freshly ground pepper

2 pounds (1 kg) ground pork

2 eggs, beaten

10 sage leaves, minced

2 yards (2 meters) pork casings (from your butcher)

2 tablespoons canola oil

MUSTARD CABBAGE

⅓ cup (80 ml) water

⅓ cup (90 g) butter

Salt

2 heads cabbage, cored and quartered

2 tablespoons coarse mustard

Garden cress or sprouts for garnish

CRISPY ONIONS

1 onion

⅓ cup (80 ml) milk

¼ cup (30 g) white spelt flour

1 tablespoon canola oil

Pickled beets and pickled cucumbers

SAUSAGES

Cook the barley in a saucepan of salted boiling water until tender, 30–40 minutes. Drain and let cool. Put the ground pork in a bowl and work in the eggs, sage, salt, and pepper with your hands. Work in the cooked barley. Fill the casings with the stuffing. In a frying pan, heat the oil and fry the sausages for 6–7 minutes on each side, or until golden and cooked through.

MUSTARD CABBAGE

Bring the water, butter, and a sprinkle of salt to a boil in a saucepan. Add the cabbage and cook until tender, 6–7 minutes. Using tongs, transfer the cabbage wedges to a bowl. Stir the mustard into the cooking water and pour over the cabbage. Garnish with cress.

CRISPY ONIONS

Cut the onion into thick slices. Pour the milk into a saucepan. Add the onion slices and cook for 3–4 minutes. Drain off the milk (reserve it for a soup or sauce). Dry the onion slices on paper towels. Coat the onion slices in the flour. Heat the oil in a frying pan and fry the onion slices until crispy.

Serve the cabbage and onions alongside the sausages, with pickled beets and pickled cucumbers.

LEFTOVERS?

HOMEMADE SAUSAGE IS AN EXCELLENT BASE FOR SAUSAGE AND EGG HASH (PAGE 146).

DUCK WITH BARLEY AND MUSHROOMS

The technique for making risotto is the basis for this dish. Instead of short-grain rice, we've substituted barley, a more nourishing Nordic grain. You might call it "barlotto."

BARLOTTO

2 tablespoons olive oil

2 shallots, minced

1 garlic clove, minced

1½ cups (250 g) pearl barley, soaked overnight

⅔ cup (150 ml) dry white wine

2½ cups (625 ml) water

1 cup (125 g) grated Parmesan cheese

⅓ cup (90 g) butter

Salt and freshly ground pepper

Fresh organic lemon juice

8 ounces (250 g) chanterelle or other mushrooms

4 celery stalks

1 tablespoon canola oil

3 duck breasts

Salt and freshly ground pepper

2 pears, halved and cored

Fresh organic lemon juice

2–3 ounces (60–90 g) blue cheese

Fresh parsley or chervil + celery leaves

BARLOTTO

In a frying pan, heat the oil over medium heat and sauté the shallots and garlic until translucent. Add the barley and let it sizzle for a minute. In a bowl, combine the wine and water. Add one-fourth of the liquid and stir until it has been absorbed; repeat until all the water has been added and the grain is tender, 20–25 minutes. The consistency of the barley should be like soft porridge. Stir in the Parmesan and butter. Season to taste with salt, pepper, and a few drops of lemon juice. Cut up the mushrooms and slice the celery thinly. In a frying pan, heat the oil and sauté the mushrooms and celery, then add to the barlotto.

Preheat the oven to 350°F (180°C).

Rub the duck breasts with salt and pepper on both sides. In a dry frying pan, over medium heat, brown the meat, fat side down, until golden brown. Turn the breasts and cook for 5–10 seconds on the second side. Transfer the duck breasts to a roasting pan and bake for 9–10 minutes. Let rest for 10 minutes. Before cutting the meat, in a dry frying pan over very high heat, give the breasts a very quick turn in the pan on the fat side, a maximum of 10 seconds, so they are seared. Slice the duck and serve over the barlotto.

Cut the pears into julienne. Drizzle with lemon juice. Divide the pear over the duck along with dots of blue cheese. Garnish with parsley and celery leaves.

EXOTIC LAMB

Close your eyes and let your senses fly you to North Africa or the Middle East.
You don't need to buy a whole leg of lamb; the boneless parts of the thigh will do.
When you grind the spices, they will release their scent and flavor.
Our version of hummus is made with ingredients easily bought at your local market.

HUMMUS

1 cup (220 g) dried chickpeas, soaked overnight

¼ cup (60 ml) olive oil

Salt and cayenne pepper

½ teaspoon ground cumin, or more to taste

Fresh organic lemon juice, to taste

TOMATO SALAD

1 tablespoon finely chopped red onion

8 ounces (250 g) small, ripe tomatoes, cut into wedges

½ tablespoons olive oil

1 tablespoon fresh organic lemon juice

Salt and freshly ground pepper

2 tablespoons thinly sliced green onions

QUINOA PANCAKES

⅓ cup (60 g) quinoa, well rinsed and drained

2 eggs

⅔ cup (160 ml) buttermilk

2 ounces (60 g) white rye flour

¼ cup (30 g) white spelt flour

1 teaspoon baking powder

2 tablespoons canola oil

LAMB SLICES

½ tablespoon *each* fennel seeds, minced fresh thyme, and ground cumin

½ teaspoon cayenne pepper

3 garlic cloves

1¼ pounds (625 g) boneless leg of lamb, sliced into 1- and 1½-inch-thick slices (3 to 4 cm thick)

2 tablespoons canola oil

Fresh cilantro leaves

1 cucumber, peeled and cut into sticks

1 head iceberg lettuce, thinly sliced

HUMMUS

Cook the chickpeas in a saucepan of lightly salted boiling water until tender; drain, saving ⅓ cup (90 ml) of the cooking water. In a bowl, mash the chickpeas with the oil and reserved cooking water. Season to taste with salt, cayenne pepper, and cumin.

TOMATO SALAD

Put the onion and tomatoes in a bowl. Add the olive oil and lemon juice; sprinkle with salt and pepper. Top with spring onion slices.

QUINOA PANCAKES

Cook the quinoa in a saucepan of salted boiling water until tender, 20 minutes. Drain and let cool. In a blender or food processor, pulse the quinoa with the eggs and buttermilk. Add the flours, baking powder, and salt and process until the batter is smooth. Let the batter rest for about 20 minutes. In a frying pan, heat the oil and cook the pancakes.

Preheat the oven to 350°F (180°C).

LAMB SLICES

Grind the spices and garlic cloves in a mortar or blender. In a bowl, work the ground mixture into the meat with your hands. Heat a cast iron or other heavy ovenproof frying pan over medium heat until hot. Add the oil, turning the pan to coat the bottom with oil. Add the thick lamb slices and cook, turning once, until nicely browned on the outside yet still very rare inside, about 5 minutes total. Transfer the pan to the oven and roast the meat for 5 minutes. Trim away the fat and cut the meat against the grain into thin slices. Place the lamb slices in a serving dish and sprinkle cilantro over the top.

Serve the lamb with the pancakes, hummus, tomato salad, cucumber sticks, and lettuce strips.

If you don't have dried chickpeas (garbanzo beans), you can use canned ones and substitute ⅓ cup of plain water for the cooking liquid. If you want to increase the nutritional value, add a little tahini (sesame seed paste). Chickpeas have only a small amount of amino acids but sesame seeds are rich in them, so the hummus will be protein-rich for the body.

SLOW-BAKED HAM HOCKS

A dinner that makes itself! After a Sunday walk, a visit to the park,
a quick visit with friends, or a gallery tour, this dish will be waiting for you
with an intoxicating aroma and rich, hearty flavors. Only the sides will need to be made.

2 celery roots, peeled and cut
into wedges

6 small apples, cored and halved
lengthwise

3 onions, cut into wedges

3 tablespoons olive oil

2 tablespoons honey

3 tablespoons apple cider vinegar

1¼ cups (310 ml) water

4 smoked ham hocks (2½ to 3 lb/
1 to 1.4 kg total)

Salt

1¼ pounds (625 g) Chinese long
beans (asparagus beans)

1 tablespoon butter

Minced fresh parsley

Preheat the oven to 350°F (180°C).

Put the celery root, apples, and onions in a nonreactive roasting pan. Mix the oil, honey, vinegar, and water in a bowl. Pour the mixture over the vegetables and season with salt. Add the ham hocks, first turning them in the fruit and vegetable mixture to coat with the liquid, and arrange on top. Transfer the pan to the oven and roast until the meat is tender, about 2½ hours. Set aside and let cool.

In the meantime, cook the long beans in a large pot of salted boiling water until very tender, 3–4 minutes. Drain. Return the beans to the pot, stir in the butter, cover the pot, and shake it.

Clean the meat off the ham hocks. Serve with the roasted apples and vegetables, long beans, and pan juices. Sprinkle with parsley.

LEFTOVERS?
MASH THE ROASTED APPLES AND VEGETABLES WITH A LITTLE BUTTER AND HEAVY CREAM. SERVE WITH PIECES OF THE HAM HOCKS. AS A SIDE, SERVE THE COLD LONG BEANS WITH SAUTÉED APPLE SLICES.

When buying pork, look for sustainably grown meat. Perhaps you will have to pay a little more, but the meat of free-ranging pigs has more flavor, and this method of husbandry is better for the environment. Cut the amount of meat per person down a bit and cook more vegetables; the price per serving will be proportionately reduced.

PIZZA

Here's a perfect plan for a fine social occasion: Make the pizza dough and tomato sauce well ahead of time. Arrange the assorted fillings and toppings on the table, so everyone can load the pizza with their favorites. One exception: Have enough rich salad greens available so that every pizza piece will have a handful.

2 packages active dry yeast (4 tsp)

1¼ cups (310 ml) lukewarm water

3 tablespoons olive oil

½ teaspoon salt

4 cups (500 g) white spelt flour

TOMATO SAUCE

¼ cup (60 ml) olive

2 garlic cloves, minced

1 onion, finely chopped

1 red chile, seeded and minced

1 tablespoon tomato paste

1 tablespoon honey

1 tablespoon vinegar

3 cups (625 g) canned or boxed chopped tomatoes

¾ cup (180 ml) water

Pinch of ground cumin

Salt and freshly pepper

3 ounces (90 g) mozzarella cheese

Choice of toppings: browned ground beef, sausage slices, smoked ham, arugula, small tomatoes, grated Parmesan cheese

Preheat the oven to 525°F (275°C).

CRUST

In a bowl, dissolve the yeast in the water. Stir in the oil and salt and enough flour to make a smooth dough. Cover the bowl with a kitchen towel and let rise until doubled, about 30 minutes. Scrape the dough out onto a floured work surface and divide into pieces. Roll out each piece and lay on a baking sheet lined with parchment paper.

TOMATO SAUCE

In a large saucepan, heat the oil and sauté the garlic, onion, and chile until the onion is translucent. Stir in the tomato paste and then add the honey and vinegar. Add the tomatoes, water, and cumin. Cover and simmer over low heat for 40 minutes. Uncover and pulse the mixture with a stick blender or in a regular blender; simmer for another 30 minutes. Season to taste with salt and pepper. Spread the tomato sauce over the rolled-out pizza crusts. Everyone can add the mozzarella and the toppings they like best. Bake at the highest possible temperature in your oven for 10–15 minutes. If using a pizza oven, bake for 7–8 minutes at 660°F (350°C).

Many people confuse the spices caraway and cumin. However, these are two different kinds of spices, with completely different flavors and aromas. Caraway *(Carum carvi)* is a traditional Nordic spice used in sauerkraut, brines, breads, and aquavit. It's indigenous to Norway and is related to carrots and parsnips. Cumin *(Cumimum cyminum)* has a much sharper flavor than caraway and is used widely in North Africa and the Middle East. It's a common ingredient in curry mixtures.

CHAPTER 5

SWEETS

FRUIT IS THE LEITMOTIF IN NORDIC DESSERTS.
ARE THERE HEALTHY DESSERTS? YES, OF COURSE.
HERE IS A COLLECTION OF SWEETS THAT CAN BE EATEN
WITH A CLEAR CONSCIENCE BOTH AFTER DINNER AND FOR SNACKS.

APPLE AND RAISIN CRUMBLE

The good thing about this dessert is that you can use any kind of apples you like, even mealy apples no one else wants.

6 apples, peeled and cored

2 tablespoons butter

¼ cup (45 g) raisins

2 tablespoons honey

Grated zest and juice of
    ½ organic lemon

1 vanilla bean, split lengthwise

CRUMBLE DOUGH

½ cup (45 g) oatmeal

⅓ cup (90 g) butter, melted

¼ cup (60 ml) honey

½ cup (60 g) white spelt flour

½ cup (60 g) almond flour

½ cup (60 g) almonds,
    coarsely chopped

Preheat the oven to 400°F (200°C).

Cut the apples into wedges. Dice the butter and mix with the apples, raisins, honey, lemon zest and juice. Scrape the seeds from the vanilla bean and stir them in. Pour the mixture into a baking dish. Lay the split vanilla pod on top.

CRUMBLE DOUGH

In a bowl, mix the ingredients for the dough until crumbly. Sprinkle the crumble evenly over the apple mixture. Bake until golden and crisp, 25–30 minutes. Serve warm.

Apples have been around since the Stone Age.
They ripen slowly in the Nordic region, but some people
maintain that it allows them to develop an especially
good flavor. Good Norwegian apple varieties are
Summer Red, Aroma, and Gravenstein.

4 SERVINGS

STRAWBERRY AND YOGURT BARS

This fresh dessert is so good that I enjoy it both for breakfast and snacks, as well as dessert.

½ cup (45 g) oatmeal

½ cup (60 g) almonds, chopped

1 tablespoon honey

¼ cup (60 g) butter

4 cups (500 g) fresh strawberries

2 tablespoons honey

¾ cup (155 g) plain Greek yogurt

Granola for sprinkling (optional)

Preheat the oven to 350°F (180°C).

In a bowl, stir the oatmeal, almonds, honey, and butter together. Spread the mixture on a baking pan lined with parchment paper. Bake until golden and crisp, 8–10 minutes. Transfer to paper towels to absorb the excess oil. Cut into bars.

Cut 2½ cups (315 g) of the strawberries into large dice. In a bowl, stir the honey into the yogurt and then fold in the diced strawberries. Let the mixture macerate in the refrigerator for 1½ hours.

Cut the remaining strawberries into wedges. Top each bar with the yogurt-strawberry mixture, some cut strawberries, and sprinkle with granola, if you like.

CHOCOLATE THINS

These are perfect to serve with coffee and can be made quickly to serve after dinner.

1 cup (90 g) almond flour

⅔ cup (90 g) white spelt flour

1–2 teaspoons unsweetened cocoa powder

½ cup (60 g) walnuts

½ cup (60 g) hazelnuts

3½ ounces (105 g) dark chocolate, coarsely chopped

1 teaspoon baking powder

1 tablespoon grated orange zest

1 vanilla bean, split lengthwise

2 eggs, beaten

¼ cup (60 ml) honey

⅓ cup (90 ml) olive oil

Preheat the oven to 350°F (180°C).

Mix together all the dry ingredients and the orange zest in a bowl. Scrape the seeds from the vanilla bean and stir them in. Stir in the eggs, honey, and oil. Spread the batter on a baking pan lined with parchment paper. Bake for 15–20 minutes. Cut into sticks, place on a baking sheet lined with parchment paper, and return to the oven for 8–10 minutes, or until dry all the way through.

Store in an airtight container.

According to medical research, dark chocolate is beneficial for both the body and the brain. Do you think that dark chocolate tastes bitter? The bitter taste is actually the medicine in the chocolate. Sensitivity to the bitter taste lessens after a few days of eating dark chocolate, so you can gradually accustom yourself to the taste in the same way as you perhaps once did with coffee.

PEARS AND OATMEAL WITH GOAT'S-MILK CREAM CHEESE

This dessert is both filling and healthy. Plus, it can be made quickly.

4 pears, peeled and cored

¼ cup (60 ml) honey

1 vanilla bean, split lengthwise

¼ cup (60 ml) apple juice

Juice of ½ organic lemon

1 tablespoon butter

CREAM CHEESE

¾ cup (180 ml) heavy cream

2 tablespoons honey

8 ounces (250 g) goat's-milk
  cream cheese, at
  room temperature

Juice of ½ organic lemon

½ cup (45 g) oatmeal

1 tablespoon honey

¼ cup (60 g) butter, melted

Granola for sprinkling

Fresh mint leaves for garnish

Preheat the oven to 350°F (180°C).

Cut the pears into large dice. Melt the honey in a saucepan and cook until it darkens. Add the pear pieces and scrape in the seeds from the vanilla bean. Cook for 3–4 minutes. Stir in the apple juice and lemon juice. Cook to reduce until almost all the liquid has evaporated. Stir in the butter.

CREAM CHEESE

In a bowl and using an electric mixer, lightly whip the cream with the honey. Blend in the cream cheese and season to taste with lemon juice.

Stir the oatmeal, honey, and butter into the cheese mixture. Spread on a baking sheet lined with parchment paper. Bake until golden and crisp, 8–10 minutes. Transfer to paper towels to absorb the excess oil. Transfer to a platter.

Serve the pears on top of the cream cheese. Top with granola and fresh mint.

Oats and barley have a special type of fiber called beta glucan. It is particularly good for the bacterial flora in your intestines. It stabilizes blood sugar, strengthens immunity, lowers cholesterol, and contributes heart-healthy antioxidants. Eat hardy oats for a healthy body.

FROZEN BERRY COMPOTE

This must be one of the world's easiest sorbets. Use your favorite frozen berries here. Beating the berries, honey, and lemon juice brings out the fructose and the consistency becomes like sorbet.

1 POUND (500 G) FROZEN RASPBERRIES
OR OTHER BERRIES
½ CUP (250 ML) + 2 TABLESPOONS HONEY
JUICE OF 1 LEMON
7 OUNCES (220 G) FRESH BERRIES
OF YOUR CHOICE

With the flat beater attachment on a stand mixer, beat the
frozen raspberries with the honey and lemon juice for 10–15 minutes.
Fold in the fresh berries and serve immediately.

Norway's fields and forests burst with both wild and
cultivated berries from June until the end of September.
Blueberries, wild raspberries, blackberries, crowberries,
and cloudberries are some of the most common
wild berries to be found.

HOMEMADE CREAM CHEESE ICE CREAM

This velvety ice cream can be made without an ice cream maker.

CREAM CHEESE

1 cup (250 g) sour cream

4 ounces (125 g) goat's-milk cream cheese

⅔ cup (160 ml) whole milk

½ cup (250 ml) honey

1½ cups (375 ml) heavy cream

CROUTONS

4 slices bread, preferably white spelt bread

2 tablespoons olive oil

Fresh blueberries

Lemon balm leaves

Preheat the oven to 400°F (200°C).

CREAM CHEESE

In a blender, combine all the ingredients and process until smooth. Pour into a shallow container and place in the freezer, stirring a couple of times as the mixture freezes.

CROUTONS

Finely cube the bread. In bowl, toss the bread in oil to coat. Spread the croutons on a rimmed baking sheet lined with parchment paper and bake until crisp, about 10 minutes.

Serve the ice cream in bowls, with the blueberries and croutons sprinkled on top. Garnish with lemon balm leaves.

LEMON CREAM

This refreshing lemon sabayon is topped with grated chocolate and
layered over toasted almonds—an unbeatable combination of flavors and textures.

LEMON CREAM

6 eggs, beaten

Grated zest of 3 organic lemons

1 cup (250 ml) fresh organic
lemon juice

1 cup (250 ml) honey

¾ cup (185 g) + 1 tablespoon cold
unsalted butter

1½ cups (185 g) raw almonds

2 ounces (60 g) dark chocolate

Preheat the oven to 400°F (200°C).

LEMON CREAM

In the top of a double boiler, combine the eggs with the lemon zest, lemon juice, and honey. Cook over boiling water, whisking constantly until thickened, 10–15 minutes. Remove from the heat and let cool for about 10 minutes. Dice the butter, add to the cream, and stir well with a spatula until the butter has melted.

Toast the almonds in a pie pan in the oven until golden and crisp, 8–10 minutes. Coarsely chop and divide among serving bowls. Pour the cream over the almonds.

Cover and refrigerate until chilled, about 2 hours. Grate the chocolate on top just before serving.

Buy organic lemons to be certain that they
haven't been sprayed; you can't wash away the
pesticides in the peel of sprayed lemons. Organic lemons
cost a little more, but you can freeze lemon zest
to have it on hand whenever you want it.

PLUM COMPOTE AND BISCOTTI

This compote can be prepared ahead of time and frozen. You can also bake
the biscotti beforehand and store them in an airtight container.

6–8 tablespoons honey

12–15 large plums

1 vanilla bean, split lengthwise

¾ cup (180 ml) apple juice

Juice of ½ organic lemon

BISCOTTI

1 cup (125 g) raw almonds

¾ cup (90 g) hazelnuts

2–3 eggs

½ cup (185 g) honey

1 vanilla bean, split lengthwise

1 cup (125 g) white spelt flour

1 cup (90 g) almond flour

Grated zest of ½ organic lemon

1 teaspoon baking powder

Preheat the oven to 350°F (180°C).

In a saucepan, melt the honey until caramelized. Halve the plums and
remove the pits. Add the plums to the honey. Scrape in the vanilla seeds
and add the apple juice. Cook until the mixture has the consistency of
porridge. Season to taste with lemon juice.

BISCOTTI

In a bowl, mix all the ingredients until the dough is firm. Roll into a
flattened log about 2 inches (5 cm) high. Place on a baking sheet lined
with parchment paper and bake until golden, 25 minutes. Remove from
the oven, leaving the oven on. Let cool slightly. Slice on the diagonal.

Return the slices to the pan and bake until crisp, 7–10 minutes longer.
Let cool.

The Norwegian plum season begins in August.
Most varieties are good for cooking. I make jelly
with plums at the peak of the season so the tasty
goodness is prolonged. Plums are packed with nutrition.

BANANA CAKE

This dessert tastes best hot or warm. If you haven't baked it right before serving, heat it up. You can also freeze it and reheat it later to serve.

¾ cup (90 g) white spelt flour

⅓ cup (30 g) almond flour

2 teaspoons baking powder

Large pinch of salt

3 large eggs, beaten

¼ cup (60 ml) honey

Grated zest of 1 organic lemon

⅓ cup (90 g) butter, melted

2 ripe bananas

1 handful slivered or chopped almonds

Preheat the oven to 350°F (180°C).

In a bowl, mix together all the dry ingredients. Make a well in the center and stir in the eggs, honey, and lemon zest. Stir in the melted butter. Pour the batter into a buttered rectangular 11-by-7-by-2-inch (28-by-18-by-5-cm) baking pan.

Slice the bananas and push them down into the batter. Sprinkle with slivered or chopped almonds. Bake for 30 minutes, or until set. Cut into squares and serve warm.

COCONUT DROPS

You just have to try this velvety confection. If any are left over, let them
sit on the kitchen counter overnight. They will taste just as good when dried.
You can serve the coconut drops with grated coconut and chocolate on top,
or dip them in melted chocolate and serve on wafer cookies.

¼ cup (60 ml) honey

¼ cup (60 ml) water

3 sheets gelatin

3 egg whites

Grated zest and juice
    of ½ organic lemon

3 tablespoons grated coconut

In a saucepan, stir the honey and water together. Boil until a light caramel
color. Dissolve the gelatin sheets in cold water for 3–5 minutes. Melt the
soaked gelatin sheets in the caramel.

Whisk the egg whites in the bowl of a stand mixer for 20 seconds. With
the mixer at full speed, pour in the gelatin mixture. Beat for 15 minutes
until the mixture has cooled. Season with lemon zest and juice; add
the grated coconut. Use a spoon to drop dollops of the mixture onto a
baking sheet lined with parchment paper.

Did you know that the "urge for sweets" is really a wrongly
interpreted desire for protein? Eat assorted nuts and
a couple bites of dark chocolate the next time the craving
for sugar hits you. Try taking a walk for 5–10 minutes,
and your desire for sweets may disappear. A few slices of
ham or bites of cheese and figs will work the same way.

BUILDING BLOCKS FOR GOOD COOKING

BERIT NORDSTRAND

HERE YOU'LL FIND A LOT TO LEARN ABOUT THE BUILDING BLOCKS

THIS BOOK IS FOR YOU IF YOU WANT TO COOK FOOD THAT CONTRIBUTES TO YOUR ENJOYMENT OF THE BEST VERSION OF YOURSELF, AS KJARTAN DESCRIBES IN THE FIRST PART OF THIS BOOK. YOU CAME INTO THE WORLD ADAPTED FOR A LIFE IN CONCERT WITH NATURE. THE FOLLOWING PAGES EXPLAIN THE CHOICES KJARTAN AND I HAVE MADE ABOUT FOOD.

If you offer your body a variety of well-chosen, pure, and carefully prepared foods, you will lay the best groundwork for good health. Well-being, satisfaction, engagement, and enjoyment are the feelings that can be created when billions of nerve cells are offered everything they need so the brain can overflow with happiness chemistry. Strength and courage are created when the body is served the necessary materials for muscle power and a strongly beating heart. Our senses are satisfied by music, art, great food, and comfortable friendships, allowing the senses and the mind to create pleasurable feelings and moods. Happy thoughts are electrical impulses in the brain cells communicating with each other. You are the world's most complicated wonder.

> **"Life isn't about finding yourself.
> Life is about creating yourself."**
> George Bernard Shaw

When you understand what your body needs to do its best job for you, you pave the way for the freshest, fittest, and happiest version of yourself. This book helps steer you there with wonderful recipes for everyday meals with health-inducing spices and herbs and fabulous desserts composed of natural foods—pure, colorful and flavorful, preferably local, and in season—for both the palate and the body. All you need to do is set aside the time to enjoy the cooking and the meals. Forget calorie counting, starvation diets, and the struggle against sweets—this is a pleasure trip that can offer stable blood sugar and a taming of your sugar urges, increased fat burning, a stable and comfortable weight, a more targeted immune defense, fewer health problems, and better moods, concentration, and memory. This is not a trendy diet, but the beginning of the rest of your life.

LIVE TODAY FOR TOMORROW IS OLD HISTORY

To promote a more enjoyable mealtime, even on a weekday, move dinner to when you can set aside a whole hour for cooking and a pleasurable meal. Set the table nicely, light the candles, and let the calm sink in. Salivate at the smell of the food as you anticipate the first bite. Sit down, taste, relax, and live. With healthy food, you'll discover rare and rich flavors.

> **"If you only do what you know you can do, you never do very much."**
> Tom Krause

> **"Raise yourself up and forgive your own history."**
> Phil McGraw

Don't be afraid to experiment with new flavors. This book brings you well-balanced meals with nutrition-rich foods that combine flavors well and create synergistic effects in the body. We offer breakfast, lunch, and dinner, and, of course, dessert. We don't believe in renunciation; instead, we focus on enjoyment and enticing health-giving natural sweeteners. For your part, open yourself to some new foods and perhaps some unexpected flavors that you could come to like. Don't be afraid of a trip to a natural-foods store, an Asian market, or a farmers' market. Put it on your calendar as a set monthly activity, and take the children or a friend along. Invite someone for coffee, for cooking together, or just for a chat. Happiness is made up of small moments of enjoyment—but they have to be created. You are the architect of your own good fortune.

Say good-bye to nutrition-poor dinners made with processed foods that give you stomachaches and blood sugar chaos and leave your body short of energy. Welcome your new, natural existence. With increased knowledge about pure foods, well-composed meals, and cooking methods that take advantage of valuable nutrition, you will see beneficial results when your body has absorbed everything it needs: the building blocks that make for a strongly beating heart, flexible muscles, a motivated and clear-thinking brain, a happy spirit, and a curiosity about life. Now, you are ready for the world's most exciting journey: the very best version of yourself.

Good luck on the journey,
Berit

USE KNOWLEDGE TO MAKE SMART FOOD CHOICES.

ENSURE THE EFFECTS OF SYNERGY WITH A VARIED CHOICE OF BUILDING BLOCKS

Our genes are suited for a life in which food is gathered and hunted. If you suddenly cut down on calories, your body is tricked into thinking that you don't have access to food. The food shortage, in combination with little physical activity, tells your body there is a crisis and to save energy. It mobilizes fewer fat cells and feverishly tries to convert all the excess energy into fat. If you offer the body a rich choice of nutritional materials that your body needs, your cell factories produce everything you need, from happy thoughts and excited hormones to stress relievers and growth hormones. Stem cells are generated from adipose tissue and become new cells for your muscles, blood vessels, heart, and bones.

Eggs contain the building blocks for a whole chicken: brain, eyes, bones, skin, and feathers. Eat eggs from hens that have grazed freely in nature.

MORE PLANT-BASED FOOD

Plants use the sun's energy when they conjoin CO_2 from the air with water they take up through their roots to produce carbohydrates. By eating carbohydrate sources from nature, such as fruit, berries, herbs, and vegetables, the sun's energy is converted to energy in your cells. Think about filling your body with solar energy just as solar panels do—you can have more just by choosing more plant-based food! Your purchases can give you more than 1,000,000 health-giving plant substances (phytonutrients), vitamins, minerals, and beneficial fatty acids. These elements together can create fine synergistic effects in your cells. The vitamins convert carbohydrates to energy, using minerals in the process and antioxidants to extinguish sparks of inflammation. You will find everything you need in nature's carbohydrate sources. I am humbled when I think about how complex and effective nature's treasures are. Vegetables, fruit, berries, spices, and herbs protect us from weight gain, diabetes, heart and cardiovascular diseases, and cancer.

Let your children go on a treasure hunt in the produce aisle and bring home a few colors from the vegetable rainbow to make the day's meals. The various colors represent different plant materials and have varying effects on your cells. A meal with several different vegetables can give you as many as 25,000 different plant elements. Most of them will extinguish sparks of inflammation (oxidants, free radicals) and are called antioxidants. They protect cell parts and mutagens against spark injuries. Other plant materials influence the reading of patterns from your genes, determine the cells' communications, and support an active and targeted immune system. If you have a great many sparks in your body and few spark-reducing plant elements, you will be ripe for increased stress, which is connected to a whole chain of health problems, mental illness, and dementia. Put out the rain of sparks with vegetables that contain nature's color splendor.

Keep in mind that it is the color inside the vegetables that counts, so red, yellow, and green apples are white unless you eat the skin. Harvest red from peppers, strawberries, and tomatoes; get orange from sweet potatoes, carrots, and cloudberries; green from broccoli, kale, and spinach; yellow from peppers, nectarines, and squash; blue and violet from figs, blue potatoes, red beets, red cabbage, blackberries, and blueberries. It is recommended that we eat at least five servings, corresponding to at least 1 pound (500 g) of vegetables, fruit, and berries every day.

Vegetables definitely produce the strongest health effects, so make four of the five servings vegetables and the fifth berries or fruit.

The flavor and color elements of plants are fat-soluble. Your saliva doesn't have any fat that can stimulate the flavors of plant-based foods in your taste buds, so help your body absorb more nutrients and stimulate your taste buds by eating good fats—butter, coconut oil, olive oil, and nut oils—with your vegetables to increase the absorption of the plant materials by several hundred percent and release the rich flavors in your mouth. A little salt and freshly ground black pepper are also beneficial so that thousands of phytonutrients will be absorbed by the body and trigger their effects where you need them most: sparking the billions of cell factories in your body into high gear.

TIPS FOR EATING MORE PLANT-BASED FOODS
- Fill half your plate with vegetables and berries—the stronger the color, the stronger the health effects. Always include something green.
- Eat fermented or fermented lactic acid greens, such as sauerkraut, pickles, and kimchi.
- Steam vegetables and serve them with garlic butter, salt, and pepper to trigger healthful effects.
- Stir-fry bok choy in oil with garlic and flavor with naturally fermented soy sauce, fish sauce, or oyster sauce.
- Sauté onions, mushrooms, peppers, and squash in a little butter over medium heat for a few minutes.
- Make a little bowl of salad or raw veggies to eat with lunch and dinner. Put vegetable sticks in the lunch box and offer veggie sticks and dip in the evening.
- Grate root vegetables and add them to tomato soup, lasagne, or taco mixes.
- Make a vegetable soup purée: two pounds (1 kg) of carrots will make enough purée for 3–4 people.
- Spread hummus (chickpeas and tahini) on bread instead of butter for variety.
- Put out some bite-sized veggie pieces and fruit while the children wait for supper to be ready.
- Make smoothies with fresh or frozen berries as an evening snack.
- Make veggie juice with carrots, overripe apples, oranges, celery, and lemon. Make red beet juice with red beets and grated ginger.
- Limit the amount of pure fruit juice to ⅓ cup (80 ml) per day, and blend with an equal amount of vegetable juice. Drink water when thirsty!
- Put two handfuls of vegetables on the plate for every handful of animal protein (meat, fish, eggs).

TIPS FOR EATING MORE LEGUMES
- Supplement ground meat with a purée of beans and lentils for meatballs and burgers.
- Add beans and lentils to lasagne, taco fillings, and pizza toppings.
- Soak legumes, such as chickpeas, lentils, and beans, in water overnight, cook them, and store them in the refrigerator. Add a little to salads, stir-fried foods, casseroles, and soups.
- Make a hummus dip with chickpeas and tahini.
- Substitute lentils, chickpeas, and beans for white rice and pasta; they will take on the flavor of any delicious sauce.

"Can it be even better?" you might be thinking. Yes, if you use legumes, seed sprouts, and fermented vegetables, you can utilize even more from nature's pharmacy. Plants come with various antinutrition elements that can both irritate the intestines and decrease the absorption of nutrients if you eat them raw. For generations, we have used techniques, such as sprouting, soaking, and fermenting, to deactivate these antinutritional elements so plants will be edible and their nutrients available to us. Modern people still use fermenting or pickling to bring out the best flavors. Fermentation converts grapes to wine and grain to beer; it turns dough to sourdough and milk to sour milk, yogurt, and cheese. Without the fermentation of cocoa beans, there would be no cocoa flavor, no coffee flavor without fermented coffee beans, and no sauerkraut, pickles, or soy sauce either. Luckily, bacterial cultures can transform indigestible and irritating plants to delicious food and also strengthen the beneficial bacteria in your intestines. Don't be lured, though, by bread with sourdough flavoring added or cabbage made sour with sugar and vinegar.

EAT ENOUGH FISH

Even though Norway is a fishing nation, we unfortunately often exclude fish as a food. We top the lists for ground beef and sausage consumption.

Many of us eat fish less than twice a week, and children and young people eat it even less often. We spend three times more money on sweets than on fish.

There are too many of us who miss the healthy benefits of fish, and it is shameful that children and young people who are growing and developing are those who eat the least fish. Fish produces more muscle mass per calorie, makes it easier to maintain a comfortable weight, lifts the spirits, and improves concentration. It can also reduce inflammation, strengthen immunity, and prevent Type 2 diabetes, heart and cardiovascular disease, cancer, depression, and dementia. It contains a considerable number of vitamin D conductors and ensures you have selenium that activates the cell's own antioxidant defenses and the iodine necessary for metabolic hormones. You must have these hormones so that your cells can regenerate, stay alive, and produce energy. Don't miss out on fish's health-sustaining powers.

Eat fish for dinner two or three times a week, and serve it as a side. The recommended amount is 10–13 ounces (315–410 grams) of fish a week. At least 7 ounces (220 g) should be a fatty fish, such as salmon, trout, mackerel, or herring. Six side portions of fish correspond approximately to one dinner serving.

TIPS FOR EATING MORE FISH

- Increase the serving size of fish to 5–7 ounces (155–220 grams) and add two fish dishes to your weekly dinner menu plans.
- Select wild fish. Try sashimi, ceviche, and partially fermented fish.
- Try dishes with salt herring. Try jarred herring in mustard sauce, or serve herring with a little chopped red onion and parsley.
- Limit the consumption of processed fish, such as fish balls, fish sticks, and fish cakes, which have small amounts of fish.
- Use fish to vary classic meat dishes: make fish burgers and wraps with salmon and smoked mackerel.
- Make salads with leftover fish and shrimp.
- Use fish bones and heads and shrimp shells to make fish stock and soups.
- Bring out umami flavor with anchovies in sauces, dips, and casseroles.
- Choose small fish that are low on the food chain—they won't have accumulated appreciable amounts of heavy metals.

REASONABLE AMOUNTS OF CAREFULLY PREPARED MEAT

Pigs, cows, and chickens that graze naturally outdoors have a large area to romp in, have access to daylight, are less stressed, and produce more nutritious meat. Hunters know that stress hormones can destroy the quality of meat, so they hunt in camouflage clothing to keep from scaring the animals. That way, they get the most tender meat with the best flavor.

Animals for human consumption should themselves feed on the best possible forage, such as grass, seeds, herbs, and insects and consume the least possible amounts of grain and soy (feed concentrate). You can find meat from pastured animals at the market, but you might have to pay a little more. Be reassured that when you consider the price per pound (kilo) in relation to good nutrition, you will have value for every penny. If you cut meat into smaller, reasonable serving sizes, the price per dinner plate will be about the same. We are a little strange: We are willing to pay a lot to live in the right neighborhood and to make sure that our children go to the best schools. That means that we will have a better quality of life. When it comes to food, though, and especially meat, we aren't as free with our money.

If you want to prepare smart meat dinners for your children, choose 100-percent high-quality meat, preferably with the skin and bones. The result will be juicy meat that is more flavorful and rich in nutrition.

Naturally raised meat gives you a staggering number of building blocks per calorie and, most of all, contributes valuable proteins, B vitamins, iron, zinc, and selenium. At the same time, those building blocks are not healthy in large amounts. The consumption of meat has increased noticeably over time, from an average of 117 pounds (53 kg) in 1989, to 168 pounds (76 kg) in 2013.

Studies by the American Cancer Society show that the risk for colon cancer can increase by 15–20 percent for every 3½ ounces (105 g) of red meat or 1¾ ounces (50 g) of processed red meat that you eat. There are various reasons for this, and ever more studies show that added nitrates and extreme heat treatments take most of the blame. But you can obtain good flavors and good health effects from naturally raised meat.

In the body, proteins in meat convert to a strong acid (urea), which must be neutralized to maintain the body's pH balance. To do that, the body uses calcium from the skeleton. To partly protect you from skeletal bone loss while you enjoy meat, drink water with some weak acid added, such as lemon or lime juice or apple cider vinegar, which is converted to alkaline in your body. Mineral-rich stock cooked from beef bones has the same effect and contains the nutrients that strengthen both articular cartilage and the skeleton. The more meat you eat, the more beef-bone stock you need to protect your skeleton from becoming weak.

Some people believe that it is a good idea to substitute tofu for meat. There were times when tofu was both rich in nutrition and fermented, necessary for breaking down dangerous soy estrogen and substances that distract the thyroid from its job. The modern, unfermented versions are processed until free of the most meaningful nutrition. In the worst case, tofu may be genetically modified. If you can find fermented soy, every bite is chock-full of beneficial nutrients.

TIPS FOR SAFELY EATING MEAT

- Select meat from naturally raised animals, preferably marbled with fat. Ask for the bones to make stock.
- Choose meat from a variety of sources: venison, moose, deer, reindeer, lamb, pig, cow, and birds. Also try dishes with liver, which is nature's vitamin shot. The liver should be considered the body's vitamin savings bank. You will also get plenty of magnesium from the chlorophyll in the plants that the animal ate.
- Calculate about 10 ounces (315 g), with a maximum of 1 pound (500 g) of red meat per person per week.
- Halve the amount of meat per serving, from 7 ounces (220 g) to 3½ ounces (105 g) and increase the amount of plant protein from broccoli, beans, lentils, nuts, and seeds.
- Vary traditional meat dishes, such as pasta, tacos, and stir-fries, by substituting fish and beans.
- Tenderize meat in sour milk.
- Marinate meat, for example, in Worcestershire sauce, olive oil, and freshly ground black pepper, for 30 minutes or overnight.
- Never cook meat taken directly from the refrigerator because you can overcook the meat before the center is cooked. Let the meat warm up on a kitchen counter for 20 minutes.
- Try different meat preparation methods: simmer in water or sous vide, bake slowly at low temperature in the oven, and frying in a pan over medium heat to get the most flavor and nutrition.

- Let cooked meat rest for 5–10 minutes before you cut it, so the valuable meat juices don't run out.
- Avoid charring meat on charcoal grills and deep-frying, which create cancer-causing toxins (heterocyclic amines and polycyclic aromatic hydrocarbons) in the meat.
- Serve meat with a sauce made with bone stock so you can retain both the collagen and minerals that benefit your connective tissue and bones.

Glucosamine is a protein in collagen that absorbs undigested matter in the intestines, travels directly to the articular cartilage, builds up new cartilage, and keeps your joints flexible. Collagen from stock bones is a necessary building block everywhere there is connective tissue, not just in articular cartilage. Bone stock and stock-based sauces contribute to building up and strengthening everything from blood vessels and bones to skin, nails, and hair. There is no reason to serve gravy only with the Sunday roast!

CHOOSE DAIRY PRODUCTS WITH NATURAL FATTY ACIDS

Milk today is not what it once was. Fresh milk from grazing animals is completely different from pasteurized, homogenized, and perhaps also fat-reduced milk from the carton. Fresh, nonpasteurized milk can build strong bones and strengthen concentration and memory and is both richer in flavor and nutrition than ultraprocessed cow's milk from the carton. Most milk is pasteurized to kill any disease-causing bacteria; even "raw" milk is partially heated. Unfortunately, we must sacrifice both protein clusters and beneficial bacteria in milk so that it will be safe for children and adults.

Protein clusters in fresh milk have precise three-dimensional structures (casein cells), that maintain their shape with the help of calcium and phosphate, which protect them against behaving as reactive minerals. When these clusters are destroyed by heating, the calcium slips free and fine clusters become long protein threads. Denatured protein threads have completely different characteristics from three-dimensional clusters, and this can be one of several reasons that many people have allergic reactions to these unnatural milk proteins.

It appears that the acidification of sour milk and yogurt helps to clear up the protein chaos so that we can use sour milk and yogurt in completely different ways from sweet milk from a carton.

I can understand why milk is heated up to protect us against illness, but I don't understand as well why dairies shatter the fragile fat globules into pieces in the milk (homogenization) just so you and I can avoid having to shake the carton before serving. These fat globules are built of membranes

similar to the walls in your cell factories. They are created by mammary cells sacrificing a little flick of their membrane when they pack in the fat droplets and send them out into the milk. These fat globule membranes have specialized antennae on the outside, just as your own cells do. These are the antennae that the beneficial bacteria in your intestines recognize and accept without immune inspection and attacks. They also stimulate the cells in the intestinal walls and stick to similar ones to absorb valuable milk fats, inhibit dangerous bacteria in the intestines, and stimulate the development of nerve cells. As long as the membranes of the fat globules are intact, the fatty acids can also shield against attacks from the calcium left from the destroyed protein clusters. If calcium and fat are allowed to react with each other, mineral absorption is weakened in the body. Homogenization leaves a battleground of shattered fat globules, destroyed antennae, reactive minerals, and long protein threads that can react with each other, and, in the worst scenario, lead to dangerous consequences for your health. Pasteurization and homogenization can convert nutrient-rich milk into a drink that leads to stomach pain, diarrhea, constipation, and significantly weakened absorption of valuable building blocks. Many people who are milk-intolerant can consume nonhomogenized acidified milk, such as kefir, on their breakfast cereal.

When I was little, I had a sweet little silver cup. Every morning, it was filled with milk, and I had to drink it all. I didn't like the taste of the milk. It seemed to be worse than cod liver oil, and, by the time I was ten, I refused to drink milk. I was told that I would have osteoporosis, but, as it happened, I may have avoided that precisely because I didn't drink milk like a calf.

For it would appear that drinking modern milk might actually lead to osteoporosis. In addition, animal research shows that galactose from split milk sugars can add to the aging process and shorten life. The intake of galactose in research animals corresponds to 1 or 2 glasses of milk for humans, with increased oxidative stress, increased levels of chronic inflammation, increased breakdown of nerve walls, a weakened immune system, and changes in the "reading" of genes. In humans, increased oxidative stress and chronic inflammation are connected with weight gain, Type 2 diabetes, mental health problems, osteoporosis, heart and cardiovascular diseases, and cancer. Studies show a higher death rate from heart and cardiovascular diseases and a greater incidence of osteoporosis and broken bones in our country with the increased consumption of milk. You should, instead, consume reasonable amounts of acidified milk products, such as cultured buttermilk, kefir, and yogurt. You will get enough calcium for strong bones this way, as from other calcium-rich sources, such as sesame seeds in their hulls, sardines, nuts, seeds, and bone broth.

Studies on humans show that higher consumption of milk can lead to higher blood pressure, lower levels of good cholesterol (HDL), and weakened effects of insulin.

The positive side is that, at the same time, studies show that consuming cheese, cultured buttermilk, and yogurt have good effects on health: increased levels of good cholesterol (HDL), better insulin effects, reduced levels of chronic inflammatory substances in the body (interleukin 6), better burning of health-endangering abdominal fat, and protection against a host of health problems, including heart and cardiovascular diseases and osteoporosis.

While acidified dairy products, such as cultured buttermilk, cheese, and yogurt, are associated with diminished oxidative stress and reduced levels of chronic inflammation in the body, regular milk is associated with increased oxidative stress and increased levels of the same types of inflammation.

What does this mean for you? It means that you can enjoy fermented or acidified dairy products, such as cheese, cultured buttermilk, kefir, and yogurt, and use cream and milk for cooking in reasonable amounts, but that you should not drink milk like a calf. Choose fermented dairy products because of their limited levels of milk sugars, easier absorption of minerals, less excitable proteins connected with allergies, strengthening effects on intestinal flora (probiotics), antioxidant power, and inflammation-reducing effects. A bowl of yogurt with berries, granola, and honey is so much better than a large glass of milk.

If you don't like dairy products or are allergic to milk proteins and are worried about getting too little calcium, make bone broth–based soups and sauces, and you will quite enjoy the rich mineral stocks in the broth and get all of the building blocks you need for strong cartilage, great teeth, and strong bones.

TIPS FOR CONSUMING MILK IN EVERYDAY FOODS

- Limit the amount of milk you drink to quench thirst.
- Choose acidified milk products such as kefir, yogurt, and cheese rather than sweet milk.
- Avoid kefir and yogurt with added sugar, artificial sweeteners, and other sugars (additives that end in "-ose" are disguised sugars).
- Choose nonhomogenized kefir if you can (with fat globules intact).
- Select milk products from pastured cows because what the cow eats affects the quality of the milk, and you will get more beneficial fatty acids in milk products from cows that graze.
- Avoid cheese made with unpasteurized milk for children and if you are pregnant because it can cause illness, but healthy adults can try it.
- If you can't tolerate cow's milk, try goat's and sheep's milks because they have completely different proteins.

FOODS FOR BALANCED INTESTINAL FLORA

The intestines are an entire world, with about one thousand different types of bacteria. They moved in and created their own society when you traveled through your mother's birth canal and were born. The bacteria from the birth canal founded this society, and new families moved in during the first hours, and perhaps days, after you were born. There are billions and billions of them, and they make up more than 90 percent of the cells in your body. You are completely dependent on these bacteria to get sufficient sustenance because they make food more nutrition rich. Beneficial bacteria convert undigested, sustenance-poor raw foods into nutrition-rich and delicious foods.

The bacteria in the intestines use a wide range of enzymes, or "scissors," that "clip" food into more absorbable bites. Then, minerals important for life, such as zinc, calcium, and magnesium from nuts, seeds, and grains, are released so that your body can absorb them and send them to the billions of hard-working cell factories. They produce their own nutrients, such as vitamins K2 and B12. At the same time, they maintain the intestinal mucosa, program the immune system, and help digestion so that food is massaged and transported farther in an appropriate consistency and in practical portions.

TIPS FOR ENRICHING AND STRENGTHENING INTESTINAL FLORA

- Eat probiotic foods with fiber and starches that keep beneficial bacteria alive, such as starch-rich root vegetables, cabbage, onions, garlic, ginger, acidified dairy products, and honey.
- Eat food that sends more beneficial bacteria to the intestines, such as fermented vegetables, berries, and fruit; fermented meat and fish; raw milk; and raw-milk cheese. You will not only gain supplies of living bacteria through such food, but the dead bacteria bodies also provide valuable nutrition in the form of smart fatty acids, proteins, vitamins, and minerals. Food is converted from partly indigestible to the purest superfood of building blocks. The bacteria also make extra building blocks for you.
- Eat a sufficient amount of fatty fish and fish oil to lubricate the internal intestinal walls.
- Let bread dough rise overnight (at least 12 hours) and soak nuts, seeds, legumes, and grain in water overnight (at least 12 hours) so the phytic acid breaks down and the minerals are ready for absorption.
- Sprout seeds so they can release, produce, and absorb considerably more sustenance. You can set out pots of sprouts on the kitchen counter and on windowsills, or invest in a sprouting cupboard the size of a little wine cabinet.

BAKE BREAD WITH ANCIENT GRAINS

Norwegians eat most meals with bread, so it is important that bread is baked with nutrition-rich whole grains. Today, whole grains represent only 20 percent of the total amount of grain products we eat. The rest is processed, free of nutrients and full of starches and gluten.

Is it worth the challenge of finding nutrition-rich bread? Yes. Choose whole-grain bread to ensure that you get both bran and germ, where all the vitamins, minerals, plant sustenance, fiber, and beneficial fatty acids live. Ask for help navigating the bread shelves at the grocery store or connect with a local baker because it's possible they have both whole-grain and wheat-free breads.

Stay away from modern wheat flour that has been crossed for generations to produce superstarches and supergluten, making industrially baked bread airy but with little nutritional material. Read the list of ingredients to have control over how much the bread will contribute meaningful nutrition and strengthen your body and brain.

If you bake your own bread, you'll have the smell of freshly baked bread in the house and full control of the ingredients and process. Do not bake bread with refined white flour but save that for cakes and cookies (refining flour eliminates 50–80 percent of the nutrition in grain that has been sowed and harvested). Instead choose ancient, more nutrition-rich types of grain, such as einkorn, emmer, farro, and spelt. These grain species have considerably more antioxidants, vitamins, and minerals; richer flavor; and less gluten. I think that I get tastier bread that stays fresh longer with these flours. Choose coarsely ground and fine-ground flour to ensure that all the nutrients remain; the kernels are only starch.

With ancient, low-gluten types of flour, make sure that you don't knead the dough too much. Work with a low speed on the stand mixer and knead the dough as if by hand. Otherwise, the dough will be sticky and the bread heavy.

We eat significantly more grain and bread than vegetables, but it really should be the opposite. Slice your bread a little thinner and serve plenty of vegetables with all-bread plates.

If you are gluten-intolerant, stay away from prepared gluten-free flour mixes that are full of starchy-rich corn flour and completely lacking in nutritional value. Instead, choose naturally gluten-free and nutrient-rich flour. Vary the flour with almonds, quinoa, coconut, buckwheat, rice, millet, legumes, and gluten-free oats.

NATURAL SWEETNESS FROM HONEY, RAW SUGARS, COCONUT SUGAR, AND MOLASSES

Instead of sugar, use natural sweeteners in cooking. Raw honey has a wonderful flavor and nutritional sustenance as well as plant material, pollen, vitamins, and minerals that combine for a whole list of documented health effects. Honey's inflammation-reducing qualities are especially important. Its antioxidant power and its ability to improve blood sugar regulation after a meal are all cited in a number of studies. Honey also fights bacteria and viruses, reduces sunburn, heals bedsores, fights sore infections, and reduces coughs better than nonprescription cough syrups. Studies of Norwegian heather honey have even shown that it can fight dangerous antibiotic-resistant bacteria. Honey strengthens beneficial intestinal bacteria, reduces the level of chronic inflammation in the body, and helps the body absorb calcium for stronger bones. Honey has earned its nickname as "nature's gold."

Honey contains twenty-five different sugar types and water, in addition to vitamins B1 (thiamine), B2 (riboflavin), B3 (niacin), B6 (pyridoxine), C, pantothenic acid, and the minerals calcium, iron, magnesium, potassium, and zinc.

You don't like honey? Try tasting different types in order to find a variety you like because honey takes on the flavor of the nectar it comes from. The sweetest honey has the most fructose, which actually tastes three times as sweet on the tongue as glucose. What's nice is that the sweetest, most fructose-rich honey also has the best moderating effect on your blood sugar because fructose must be converted through many links; it is absorbed slowly in the intestines and can be converted to fat more easily than blood sugar.

Refined white sugar and artificial sweeteners are found in many processed and semiprocessed products without our being aware of them—not just in juice, jam, cookies, and soda, but also in foods that we think are healthy. Yogurt can have more added sugar than a soda, meat can be marinated with sauces sweeter than chocolate sauce, and breakfast cereals might have more sugar than cakes. It isn't the sweetness that is the problem, it is the refining and production of the sweeteners that make them an unnatural food for the body. Refined sugar is stripped of the vitamins, minerals, and plant material that should be available when sugar burns into energy in your cells. Nature has figured that out and dispatches a full package — everything that is needed so the sweetness of honey, maple syrup, coconut flowers, dates, and good ripe bananas can create a symphony of synergistic effects in your body.

Studies show that artificial sweeteners also promote poor health. Even if the producers of artificial sweeteners and low-calorie soda contend that it hasn't been demonstrated that people have gotten cancer from artificial sweeteners, rats and mice have. Artificial sweeteners can induce increased absorption of sugar from the intestines, the urge to eat sweets, weight gain, lowered insulin sensitivity, Type 2 diabetes, high blood pressure, metabolic syndrome, and weakened concentration, which happens because a brain anesthetized by strong artificial sweeteners is no longer stimulated sufficiently by natural sweetness. That means that you have even stronger cravings for sweetness in order to be satisfied. Artificial sweeteners, which have been considered an easy way to prevent weight gain, are therefore a "wolf in sheep's clothing."

TIPS FOR SUBSTITUTING HONEY FOR SUGAR IN RECIPES

- Use ¼ cup (60 ml) honey for ⅓ cup (9 g) sugar, and a little more than ⅓ cup (80 ml) if you are baking with honey, to slightly reduce the sweetness.
- Add ½ teaspoon baking powder to baking recipes for every ¾ cup (180 ml) honey you are using to compensate for honey's low pH (3.2–4.5).
- Grease the measuring cup with a little oil before measuring honey so it will pour out easily.
- Get solid honey to flow by heating it up to 105°F (40°C). Don't let the temperature go above 105°F (40°C) or the healthy aspects of honey will be destroyed. Look for honey that hasn't been heat-processed, or ask for raw honey.

TIPS FOR NATURAL SWEETNESS IN EVERYDAY FOODS

- Avoid foods that have added sugar and sweeten the food yourself. This also applies to products sweetened with fructose, maltose, lactose, high fructose syrup, and glucose.
- Buy various sources of natural sweetness: heather honey, linden honey, flower and berry honey, maple syrup, molasses, coconut sugar, raw cane sugar, etc.
- Buy natural foods, such as dark chocolate (higher than 80 percent), nuts, coconut, coconut oil, dates, figs, apricots, oatmeal, almond flour, etc., from which to make desserts.
- Plan evening snacks or desserts for every evening so you can avoid being hit by cravings for sweets.
- Use naturally sweet yogurt and Greek yogurt with honey.
- Make sweet smoothies with fully ripened bananas and pears.
- Instead of soda, drink carbonated water with lemon, lime, or a little freshly pressed juice.
- Make your own breakfast cereal and sweeten it with honey.
- Buy naturally raised meat and make the marinade yourself.

CHOOSING THE RIGHT FATS

Previously we believed that saturated fat and cholesterol in food were dangerous because they lodged in the arteries and hastened heart and cardiovascular diseases. In fear of illness, we lived on fat-reduced food and margarine from plant material. Now it has been shown that it is precisely that fat phobia and lean food that can contribute to weight gain, Type 2 diabetes, and heart and cardiovascular disease. In studies of saturated fats in the 1960s, researchers used artificially produced saturated fats (hydrogenated plant oils) instead of natural saturated fats from butter, meat, and coconut oil. Studies of such artificial saturated fats showed that they caused heart and cardiovascular diseases. The researchers generalized and advised against all types of saturated fats and cholesterol in food. The food industry threw itself into promoting lean, fat-reduced, and highly processed products of all sorts. At the same time, we advised patients to cook lean meat, to spread margarine on bread, to choose low-calorie, tasteless cheeses, to drink skim milk, and to eat eggs only on Sundays. The incidences of heart and cardiovascular diseases rose higher than ever before. Today we know that the innocent suffered for the guilty. It was artificial fats, sugar, and starches that created blood sugar chaos, abdominal fat, inflammation, and sickness. Nature doesn't make dangerous fats—but it is dangerous to be without fat. Our billions of cell factories need steady deliveries of fat to maintain production.

The visible fat in foods, such as marbling in a steak or olive oil in the bottle, is composed of triglycerides, phospholipids, and cholesterol. These, in turn, are constructed of fatty acids that are either straight and saturated or zigzag-shaped and unsaturated. Monosaturated fatty acids have one kink, while polysaturated fats have several kinks. Fats in different raw foods consist of larger or smaller amounts of saturated, unsaturated, or polyunsaturated fat. Olive oil, for example has the highest number of fatty acids, with one kink in the shape of omega-9; fish oil is rich in polyunsaturated fatty acids of the type omega-3 (EPA, DHA); while coconut oil offers the saturated fatty acid called lauric acid. Reasonable amounts of natural saturated fats are necessary for normal cell function.

Carefully choose pressed oils from olives, nuts, and coconut. These are oils humans have used for generations. Always select cold-pressed oils because they contain high-quality fatty acids. They are rich in color, have strong flavors, and are rich in phytonutrients. They cost a little more, so it is important that you don't destroy the fatty acids by heating them up in the pan or oven. Except for the best-quality cold-pressed canola oil, steer clear of oils pressed from plants, so-called vegetable oils. They are refined and heated so that they come with destructive fatty acids that can cause health problems. Studies have shown that vegetable oils are connected with weight gain, Type 2 diabetes, inflammation, heart and cardiovascular disease, mental health problems, and cancer. Those fats that are healthy in seeds are not as healthy in the jar.

TIPS FOR INCLUDING REASONABLE AMOUNTS OF THE RIGHT FATS

- Choose extra-virgin olive oil (2 tablespoons per day recommended); cold-pressed canola oil, peanut oil, flaxseed oil, walnut oil, sesame oil, wheat germ oil, or coconut oil (1 tablespoon per day recommended).
- Spread butter on bread and vary that with hummus or mashed avocado.
- Sauté in clarified butter or animal fat on medium heat and add herb sprigs for extra flavor and to keep the oils from oxidizing.
- Avoid prepared salad dressings. Make your own with extra-virgin olive oil.
- Avoid vegetable oils in foods such as chocolate, cookies, salad dressings, breakfast mixes, cakes, muffins, and commercially made bread.

FATS FOR FRYING

Canola oil has the ideal balance of polyunsaturated fats and monounsaturated fat and is rich in omega-3 fatty acids. The heart-healthy fatty acids in rapeseed oil are not destroyed in the frying pan if you don't turn the heat too high. It can tolerate temperatures all the way to 350°F (180°C). Coconut oil is another source of fat that tolerates high temperatures. It contributes medium-length saturated fatty acids that the body can use.

NATURAL SALT IN REASONABLE AMOUNTS

Salt enhances the flavor in almost every dish. The minerals in salt can also help to regulate body temperature, conduct electric impulses into nerve cells, and maintain fluid balance. The salt balance in our bodies is so exacting that we have our own thermostats, alarm systems, and hormones to keep the salt concentration in the blood stable, even when our intake varies. When the salt intake exceeds a sensible level and nears 1,000 percent more than needed, advanced regulatory mechanisms break down.

On average, we eat a dangerous level of ½ teaspoon (10 g) of salt every day, 6–7 times more than we need (1.5 g) and more than double the amount that the body can use (¼ tsp/5 g) over time.

Much of the salt you consume every day is hidden in the food you eat. Yes, fully 75 percent of the salt comes from commercially prepared, ready-to-eat food, with bread and meats having the most salt.

When you buy salt at the store, choose natural salts rather than table salt. Table salt contributes only the minerals sodium and chloride, while salts such as sea salt, Maldon flaky sea salt, and Himalayan salt, have many more of the minerals that your cells need.

It is recommended that salt intake be limited to a maximum of ¼ teaspoon (5 g) a day, and even less for children. You will notice that your "need for salt" will decrease once you become used to eating a smaller amount.

TIPS FOR REDUCING YOUR SALT INTAKE

- Sprinkle lemon or lime juice, freshly ground pepper, and various types of vinegar, such as white wine or spiced vinegar and balsamic, on your food.
- Choose fresh or dried herbs, such as oregano, basil, and parsley, and spices of all kinds to replace salt.
- Use onions, garlic, and chiles that have strong flavors and also enhance the flavors of other foods.

TEACH YOUR CHILDREN TO LIKE EVERYTHING

We experience flavors differently. I've definitely had experience with that, with six children in the family. Research shows that the foundation for our taste preferences was laid long before we took our first step.

Did you know that a fetus smells what the mother is eating and drinking? The baby in the uterus swallows more fetal water if the mother drinks more sweet drinks than if the mother consumes something bitter. Infants seem to prefer flavors and smells that they have experienced in the womb.

The simple foods we were introduced to before the age of seven months are easier for us to like, so give children a varied choice of flavors and textures before they are seven months old, when they are the most flexible in their tastes. From the age of two, we develop a healthy skepticism that affects our choice of foods. I believe we were created this way so that we wouldn't eat everything we came across as we were learning to feed ourselves.

Studies have shown that children can learn to like flavors they don't like initially. While infants can quickly learn to like new flavors, you have to be a little more patient with older children. When a child is two years old, it might be necessary to make five to ten attempts to like a food. One study of children aged two to six showed that parents try only three to five times to get a child to eat a food. A succession of studies supports the contention that each taste of a food increases eventual acceptance.

If they don't like a food, such as broccoli, don't give up. Try both mashed and steamed, with

and without butter. Children's taste experiences change every time they try broccoli in their mouth. After five to ten attempts, broccoli will be perceived as something safe, and the child will recognize the flavor and react less or not at all. Reward children when they try new flavors. At our house, the reward is an activity. Let the child wish for an activity they love, such as a trip to the swimming pool, an afternoon on the climbing wall, mother and father in the sandbox, the whole family at the skating rink or soccer field. Write the prize down on a chalkboard hanging on the kitchen wall. Every time the child has tasted something new, draw a star on the board. After five to ten stars, the activity is awarded. This method shifts the attention from "Do you like this?" to "I want to have a prize," and you will have accomplished a goal: your family will eat more varied foods and will be more active together. At our house, we collect the stars for another trip to the swimming pool.

Some people tolerate bitter flavors, such as arugula, legumes, and dark chocolate, better than others. We are actually equipped with a variety of taste buds that register the bitter taste. At our house, two of us tolerate bitter herbs, leafy greens, and legumes the least. To camouflage bitter flavors, I add both acidity and sweetness when I mix a fresh vinaigrette for salads or add strong flavors like grated ginger and lemon juice to a smoothie. I use the stick blender to purée lentils, chickpeas, and beans so they can disappear out of sight in sauces.

Are you or your children among those who usually want something sweet and would prefer to avoid the salad bar? Do you have children who pick through their food and are satisfied only when they are served pizza, cereal, or pancakes? Studies show that fat- and sugar-rich foods, such as french fries, pizza, chips, and candy, are most liked, and vegetables are least liked. You cannot turn back time, but you can give the whole family a fresh start. Introduce new foods and unexpected textures combined with a cozy setting and family closeness.

Did you know that a lack of minerals can change a flavor experience, so that delicious flavors no longer taste good? Modern humans are more vulnerable to mineral deficiency due to, among other causes, modern farming, with fewer nutrition-rich plant varieties, harsh processing, and the refining of foods leading to the loss of minerals on the way to your dinner plate. Additionally, we must produce unnatural amounts of insulin for the rapid absorption of carbohydrates from white bread, pasta, and fast food that has added sugar. When your pancreas produces insulin in excess amounts, your zinc levels decrease because zinc is one part of the insulin molecule. Zinc deficiency can lead to the development of an aversion to flavors in natural foods and a desire for increased starchy, calorie-laden, and sustenance-poor alternatives. Break this bad food cycle by making sure you eat natural foods and a wealth of minerals from vegetables, sprouts, nuts, and seeds.

In order to have peace during dinner and enjoy family togetherness, you might move dinner to a time of the day when you can devote an hour to cooking and enjoying food. The body cares more about getting a choice of building blocks than what time it is!

Let your children help with the cooking. Studies show that children will more readily taste and like foods they've prepared themselves. Spread an oilcloth on the floor and move the prep there. A two-year-old loves to break carrots, tear salad leaves, and squeeze the juice out of a half lemon.

CONTRIBUTING FACTORS TO FOOD AVERSIONS AND THE URGE FOR EMPTY CALORIES

- It appears that degraded protein snippets in the intestine from masses of milk proteins and gluten can affect the pleasure center in the brain. In sensitive brains, protein snippets can disturb both attention and concentration. Because the same snippets trigger enjoyment and well-being in the brain, an urge for food high in gluten and milk solids follows. It is exactly those who have a severe milk intolerance who often stand in front of the refrigerator and drink a quart.
- Food additives, such as monosodium glutamate (MSG), can disturb flavor experiences. MSG can be found, for example, in bouillon cubes, meat spreads, and inexpensive soy sauce (choose the more expensive kind, which is naturally fermented).

Practice makes perfect. Just think about when you first began drinking coffee. The first cup tasted disgusting, but now you can't do without it. Serve the same food to the children and the adults at the table with the rule that you have to at least taste each food, but you don't have to eat it all.

TIPS FOR GETTING CHILDREN TO EAT HEALTHY AND VARIED MEALS

- If you are pregnant, eat a variety of natural plant-based foods, such as vegetables, legumes, nuts, and seeds. This allows the fetus to become familiar with a variety of flavors while in the womb.
- Don't purée all the food to help children learn to accept different textures. However, don't make the textures too different. Clumps in a thin soup might be less tolerated than clumps in a thick vegetable purée.

- Separate the flavors rather than serving everything blended in a glass. That way, a child will learn to like and recognize different pure flavors.
- Offer a child more vegetables that you prepare fresh at home. A study in the United Kingdom showed that children who had such vegetables often ate more kinds of vegetables by seven years of age than those who had prepared puréed vegetables from a jar.
- Let children feed themselves as early as possible. By five to six months, more than half of children can sit and have enough head control to grab food and feed themselves. Checking out the food and feeding themselves stimulates the development of taste and large and small motor movements. Well-cooked broccoli, carrots, or another vegetable, fruit, or small pieces of bread sticks dipped in a soft-boiled egg are fine. From small acorns, great oaks grow.

TIPS FOR LEARNING TO ENJOY NEW FLAVORS

- Avoid refined white foods, such as sugar, modern wheat flour, white rice, and pasta.
- Choose pure, natural foods that do not have the additive MSG.
- Make up a fun name for dishes, for example, "Ugly Soup" for a vegetable soup and "Shrek Smoothie" for a green smoothie.
- Don't mix foods on the plate. Children like to keep flavors separate.
- Reward children and everyone in the family when they try new flavors.

TIPS FOR DISGUISING NEW FLAVORS

Pasta Sauce

Hide a vegetable purée or mashed beans and lentils in pasta sauce, using four times as much pasta sauce as vegetable purée. A stick blender mixes everything well. Try root vegetables, including sweet potatoes, and legumes. Gradually make the vegetables more visible as the flavors become more accepted.

Soups

It's amazing how many vegetables, beans, and lentils you can hide in a good soup—particularly when you have a stick blender.

Muffins

Try chicken, vegetable, and fruit muffins.

Pancakes

Add puréed sweet potatoes to the batter or add grated greens to the frying pan before you add the batter.

Peanut Butter

Mix in hummus, other nuts, or puréed beans, lentils, or chickpeas to the peanut butter.

Meatballs

Supplement ground beef with lentils, beans, chickpeas, or a little grated root vegetable. Make a lot of meatballs and freeze them. They thaw easily in the lunch box!

Juice

You can make juice with a little bit of vegetable, fruit, and berries and mix that with freshly pressed or squeezed fruit juice. Carrot juice is good in both juice and smoothies.

Smoothies

Make green berry smoothies by mixing in a bit of greens from plants. Cucumber, celery, mild lettuce, beans, lentils, avocado, and so on can be blended with the flavors of fruits and berries that you like a lot. Use a maximum of 40 percent greens and a minimum of 60 percent fruit and berries. If you add a little flaxseed oil to the smoothie, you'll also get omega-3 (ALA) fatty acids.

Chocolate Balls

Buy raw chocolate powder and mix it with a little coconut oil and an assortment of nuts, seeds, coconut, and other goodies to make chocolate balls that will count as a vegetable.

Breakfast Cereal

Crush or grind nuts and seeds to strew over breakfast cereal for extra nutrition. We usually have a few nuts roasted in organic maple syrup to sweeten our oatmeal.

If this all seems to be quite challenging, moderate your goals for a while. The setting of mealtime is important, and the mood shouldn't be destroyed by cell phones and iPads. Try shifting the goal away from eating for a time and switch to letting your child watch a favorite program on TV. The positive feeling the child will have as a result can draw attention away from the new food. You'll see—it works!

SAVING NUTRITIONAL ELEMENTS BY VARYING PREPARATION METHODS WHEN PREPARING GOOD NATURAL FOODS

Modern species of plants are crossed to produce a maximum yield plus a lack of crop rotation, rough handling of the earth, fertilizing, and spraying have noticeably decreased the levels of nutrients in vegetables and fruit since the 1940s and 1950s. This means that today's vegetables, fruit, and berries have up to 40 percent fewer vitamins and minerals than previously. When consumers choose unsprayed, carefully processed, and local foods, those foods can have increased nutritional value and flavor. When you decide to pay a little extra for organic and local foods, it is crucial that you don't destroy the advantages you've paid for when you prepare and cook the food. How well your body will benefit from nutrition is affected by how foods are stored, prepared, and enjoyed.

Not all nutrients are absorbed and used as well in the body. We call that difference bioavailability. It is nice that we can increase the bioavailability of nutritional materials and ensure that more smart building blocks make it all the way to our cell factories that need them. We can influence the offerings of smart building blocks to the cells by optimal cultivation, harvesting, preservation, careful processing, and preparation of food. A little beneficial fat in a salad and in the frying pan, freshly ground pepper on the food, and lightly steamed vegetables can improve bioavailability of the nutritional materials you sorely need.

Generally speaking, the absorption of nutritional materials, such as carbohydrates, proteins, and fat, is good (about 90 percent), while the absorption of micronutrients such as vitamins, minerals, and plant substance can vary considerably.

According to the World Health Organization, sufficient consumption of fruits and greens could save as many as 2.7 million lives every year. The storage of vegetables after harvesting can result in the loss of nutrition if weeks and months go by. If you store vegetables in a cool, dark place, such as the refrigerator, you will gain a 10 percent increase in the beta-carotene in carrots during the first two weeks after harvesting. However, researchers have found a loss of beta-carotene by 10 percent in green beans after 16 days in storage. If you freeze spinach, peas, and broccoli in season, you can even increase the levels of nature's plant power. Eat fresh fruit before it becomes overripe and the pectin breaks down. Pectin in the plant cell walls glues the plant cells together and imparts a delicious crisp consistency in fruit such as apples, peaches, plums, citrus, gooseberries, cranberries, and grapes, and to vegetables such as carrots, tomatoes, peas, and potatoes. Pectin starts the process of digestion, strengthens the bacteria in the intestines that protect you against illnesses (overweight, diabetes, heart disease, and cancer), and binds to cholesterol and sugars in the intestines, reducing the absorption of both. The expression "An apple a day keeps the doctor away" seems particularly valid. Ensure that you get pectin fiber by eating fruit before it gets too ripe and the pectin is lost.

You can find sufficient pectin in citrus zest. Buy organic citrus fruits, such as oranges, lemons, and limes, grate the zest, and use it in food. Dry or freeze grated zest so that you'll always have some on hand when you need it later on. Mix bits of pectin-rich, small, unripened apples, some cranberries, or a little grated orange zest into uncooked jam with strawberries, which have low levels of pectin. Pectin thickens the jam and gives it a fresher flavor.

Careful cleaning of vegetables and fruit is the best safeguard for retaining fiber content. Even if the fiber from plant cells is digested to a limited degree in humans, it contributes insoluble fiber with nutrients to the bacterial flora in the intestines, which aids digestion and strengthens health. Because our fiber intake is well below the recommendation of .88–1.2 ounces (25–35 g) per day, it is important to avoid destroying the fibers when processing and preparing raw foods. While juicing and filtering fruit and berries remove the most valuable fiber, you can get everything you need if instead you process whole fruit in a blender and drink it as a smoothie. Don't remove the fiber-rich peel on fruits and greens that shouldn't be peeled.

In a study on peas, researchers found a 25–35 percent higher fiber content in cooked frozen and canned peas than in cooked fresh peas. Different types of peas can be one explanation. For green beans, it was the opposite: the cooked beans won on fiber. According to the USDA Nutrient Database, peeled and canned peaches have the same fiber as peeled fresh peaches. Again, though, watch out for added sugar in canned fruit, and buy only those products that have natural, unsweetened juice.

Serve dishes that are visually appealing and chew your food well. An attractive table and the enticing smell of food pave the way to the production of digestive juices, hence the saying, "the mouth waters." Long chewing cuts up the food well and makes it more available for digestive enzymes in the mouth, stomach, and duodenum.

The removal of antinutritional materials in foods increases the absorption of nutrients. Such antinutrients can bind the sustenance in the intestines and prevent the nutrient material from being transported into the body. Or, they can compete over the same transportation system, so that less nutrition is absorbed. Phytic acid in legumes and grains, nuts and seeds is one of those antinutrient materials that reduces the absorption of calcium, iron, and zinc. Soaking peas, beans, and nuts; lengthy rising or fermentation of grains; and sprouting legumes and seeds eliminate much of that acid. Soak legumes overnight, and let dough rise for 12 hours or more so that most of the phytic acid is removed and the absorption of nutrients is increased .

Individual factors can influence the absorption of nutrition in the body. The absorption of B12 is affected by the level of stomach acid (HCl) in the stomach and the amount of protein (R-protein and IF=intrinsic factor) that help B12 through the intestinal wall and into the body. All this is produced by cells in the mucous membranes in the stomach. As you age, the mucous membranes weaken, production slows, and absorption of B12 is considerably reduced.

It appears that the body, to a certain degree, can increase the absorption of calcium and zinc when it needs to (such as during pregnancy), while, at the same time, illnesses, such as inflammation and infections, can actually lessen nutritional absorption as the body fights against the illness, when nutritional need is greatest.

The way you prepare food also influences the absorption of vitamins, minerals, and plant materials from food. A good example is that heating carrots, spinach, and tomatoes increases the absorption of the orange-red color substances (carotenoids) in the body. Actually, the absorption of lycopene increases up to 600 percent when you heat tomatoes. For that reason, it's good that almost 80 percent of all tomatoes enjoyed in the USA are in the form of packaged tomatoes that have been heat-processed. Studies show that canned tomatoes can actually have more available vitamin E and carotenoids than fresh tomatoes. Some of the variation can, of course, be attributed to the choice of tomato types that are rich in those color substances. Watch out for added sugar and salt in canned fruit and vegetables. Choose those canned in their natural juice.

We prepare foods with various methods such as boiling, sautéing, and stir-frying based on flavor, ease, consistency, and color more than how the method preserves the nutrition in the food. Studies show that about 70 percent of us fill a saucepan with cold water, add the vegetables, bring the water to a boil, and boil, for example, carrots or broccoli for 6–10 minutes. Instead, placing the vegetables in a steamer and letting them steam over rapidly boiling water for only 3–5 minutes is the best way to conserve the valuable nutrition in the vegetables.

Different preparation methods can cause vegetables to lose vitamins, minerals, proteins, and plant material, such as carotenoids, polyphenols, and glucosinolates. If you want to heat food, a light steaming is far better for retaining the nutritional value. Studies of broccoli have shown that the chlorophyll content is decreased by 18–23 percent when stir-fried and up to 27 percent when boiled, while steaming allows the chlorophyll content to remain almost unchanged and is also the best way to preserve the proteins and soluble fiber. Boiling and stir-frying reduced vitamin C content dramatically, while steaming showed unchanged vitamin C content when compared with raw broccoli. Steamed broccoli has just as much vitamin C as raw! An exception to the rule is the orange-red color substances, carotenoids, which seems to increase in boiled or steamed broccoli compared with raw. If you decide to sauté broccoli in a pan, you might also lose as much as 67 percent of these plant substances, which are believed to protect us from cancer. If you want to ensure that you get those carotenoids, steam the vegetable over a little water. Use that water when you make vegetable purée so you will also get the carotenoids that leached out into the cooking water. The same applies to making purée out of other vegetables such as carrots, sweet potatoes, and rutabaga. Steam them and then use the boiled water for the purée.

In Europe and the United States, carrots contribute about 50 percent of all the beta-carotene we get. If you steam or boil them, it won't affect the consistency in an appreciable way, but the cooking time is more crucial. Steaming leads to appreciably less loss of beta-carotene than boiling and also gives the carrots a fresher color. Both steaming and boiling increase the level of beta-carotene by, respectively, 142 percent and 130 percent. This is due to the increased release from ruined carrot cells after heat treatment. If you boil them too long, the released beta-carotene is broken down. After 20 minutes, steaming showed still increased levels of available beta-carotene (+40 percent), while the loss was obvious with boiling for 20 minutes (-19 percent) and 30 minutes (-40 percent). So, steam carrots in a steamer and save the boiled water. The orange color you see in the water indicates valuable nutrition!

Newer studies on celery have shown that steaming 10 minutes) versus boiling (10 minutes) or blanching (3 minutes in boiling water and then plunged into ice water) was superior for preserving the polyphenol level. For both boiling and blanching, up to 41 percent of the polyphenols were lost, while steamed celery had 83–99 percent of the polyphenols intact compared to raw celery.

Glucosinolates are perhaps the strongest plant material in broccoli when it comes to programming immunity and defenses against cancer. They are water-soluble, sulfurous connectors that you also find in cauliflower, cabbage, brussels sprouts, and kale. Both the preparation methods and processing of broccoli before cooking affect the amount of glucosinolates you will get. If you cut broccoli into pieces before you boil it, the enzyme myrosinase is brought into contact with the plant matter and the process of breaking down proceeds quickly. The process continues well if you eat the vegetables the same way. Chewing, cutting, and heating activate the conversion of glucosinolates to active plant matter that protects you (isothiocyanates). If you cook the vegetables a few hours after cutting them up, you will, however, lose considerable plant power.

Studies from the Netherlands have shown that steaming broccoli can increase the level of glucosinolates (+17 percent), but you lose considerable amounts of the health-giving plant matter if you boil vegetables. A study showed that a short cooking time preserved the sweetness and disguised the bitter taste best and imparted the freshest green color.

Blanching, boiling, and microwaving decrease the levels of glucosinolates in vegetables, while steaming, as some studies have shown, actually increases the level of glucosinolates. Steaming and stir-frying (in good oil for 3–5 minutes) at a high temperature (400°F/200°C) safeguards the glucosinolates best in broccoli, brussels sprouts, cauliflower, kale, and cabbage. Cook for as short a time as possible to retain the chewing resistance in the vegetables.

Cool the water used for steaming and save it in the refrigerator to add to sauces, soups, juice, and green smoothies.

The greener and crunchier a broccoli floret is after preparation, the better preserved are the chlorophyll and pectin. When chlorophyll and pectin break down, florets become a bland olive-green and completely lose their crunch. Salt in the steaming water and the shortest possible heat processing before broccoli is plunged for a moment in ice water best preserves the freshness. This is a well-known method in restaurants, because a meal should be a pleasure for both the eyes and the palate, and it is wonderful that the method also appears to best preserve the nutrients.

The mineral content of vegetables is also preserved well by blanching (3 minutes in boiling water, then into ice water) and, in studies, measured 78–91 percent of the mineral content of raw vegetables. You will probably also have a very small mineral loss when heating destroys the cell walls in vegetables so the minerals can be more easily absorbed in the intestines. The mineral content of the cooked food can also be affected by the water quality where you live. Vegetables can actually absorb calcium from water if you steam them over hard water.

Snap and break vegetables by hand instead of using a knife, so that the plant divides along its natural separation lines and the cells of the vegetables are not destroyed. The next time you make salad, tear the lettuce leaves by hand instead of cutting them with a knife!

The composition of a meal can also contribute to increased uptake of building blocks from the food basket. Absorption of the orange-red carotenoids from tomatoes, squash, and carrots is a good example. Because the carotenoids are fat soluble, the intake in your body increases if you have a little fat (3–5 grams) in a serving of vegetables. Lycopene, one of the strongest carotenoids, is best at preventing cancer cells from dividing and is better absorbed in your body when you add a few drops of olive oil to tomato slices. Beta-carotene in carrots and squash streams into your body better with a spoonful of butter in carrot purée and a splash of cream in squash soup.

All fat-soluble nutritional materials, such as fat-soluble vitamins and plant matter, are better absorbed by your body if a meal contains fat, for example, lutein in spinach, kale, broccoli, and green peas. Wedges of egg and cheese cubes in salads, and a little whole-fat Greek yogurt in smoothies also help. Another example is the absorption of iron. Iron is found as heme iron or nonheme iron in food. Heme iron is found only in animal sources with hemoglobin and myoglobin, the iron molecules protected by the protein cluster heme. In the intestinal mucosa, you have your own transport system that lifts these clusters into the body and ensures an effective absorption of iron. Plants have a type of nonheme iron that is less well absorbed. If you combine iron-rich raw foods with ingredients that are rich in vitamin C, the latter will triple the iron absorption in your body.

TIPS FOR COMBINING FOODS FOR PEAK NUTRITION
- Serving citrus fruit with spinach increases the absorption of iron from the spinach.
- Heating tomatoes changes the lycopene to a more easily absorbable form.
- Boiling carrots breaks down the cell walls and makes the beta-carotene available for absorption in the intestines.
- Drizzling oil on green salad leaves increases the absorption of lutein.

The best way is not necessarily devouring everything raw. Heating can kill bacteria in food, open plant cells, and make nutrients easier to absorb in the intestines. Steaming has advantages over boiling. You lose some fragile vitamins in order to win more plant substance. If you vary your preparation methods, add a little good-quality fat, and top it all off with freshly ground pepper, you will ensure both magical flavors and plant power.

ABOUT OILS AND FATS

Plant oils are extracted by the mechanical pressing of rapeseed, olives, nuts, and seeds. Oil bottled directly, cold-pressed or extra-virgin, retains its natural color and flavor and an array of well-preserved beneficial fatty acids and plant nutrients. Do not destroy them with heating but, instead, use them in vinaigrettes and to drizzle on salads and cooked foods.

To produce a higher smoke point, oil is refined industrially. Various methods are used, such as bleaching, filtering, and extraction with high heat. The result is a flavor-neutral oil that has a long shelf life and tolerates high temperatures in the frying pan. Clarified butter is processed along the same principles, as the milk solids are removed when the butter has melted. This raises the smoke point. Clarified butter is also easier to tolerate if you are milk protein—intolerant.

If you have spent extra money on high-quality ingredients in order to obtain the great building blocks your body needs, it is imperative that the nutrition and flavor not be destroyed in the frying pan or oven by temperatures that are too high. We want the beneficial fatty acids in the cold-pressed coconut oil to reach the brain and contribute to better concentration and memory and not be destroyed in the cooking process.

Choosing the right fat for cooking can be a challenge because we have so many oils to choose from. On the one hand, you want an oil that can tolerate the cooking temperature you need without being destroyed. On the other hand, you want an oil with the best omega-3/omega-6 balance and that has a high level of omega-9s to protect against overweight, diabetes, heart disease, and cancer. Even better is an oil rich in plant energy in the form of antioxidants and vitamins.

Whatever oil you choose, know what its smoke point is. The smoke point is the highest cooking temperature the oil tolerates before it is destroyed, which can be dangerous for you. High temperatures quickly convert beneficial unsaturated fatty acids into hardened and partially hardened health-endangering substances. In addition, overheated oil can release toxins and dangerous sparks or free radicals.

TIPS FOR CHOOSING AND USING OILS

- Buy organic, unrefined, cold-pressed plant oils such as extra-virgin olive oil, cold-pressed canola oil, and cold-pressed coconut oil. Both canola and olive oil have somewhat more omega-6s than omega-3s, but they give you a nice bonus in the form of more monounsaturated fat (omega-9s).
- Know the enemies of food oils: light, air, and heat. Cooking adds dangerous elements to oil, so it must be stored in a dark place in an airtight container. Olive oil is a fresh food and should be enjoyed while fresh.
- Choose oils in dark bottles. Frosted bottles filter out 60 percent of the light rays. Do not transfer the oil to a translucent serving jar that stands on the dinner table.
- Do not reuse heated oil.
- Check to make sure the oil's best-by date has not passed. An expensive oil might have been at the store for a while.
- If you have a large bottle of oil, transfer the contents to smaller bottles and store in the refrigerator.
- The color of olive oil shows only when the olive fruits were harvested and says nothing about the quality.
- Sniff the oil, and if it smells like machine oil, it is rancid and should not be used.
- Always wash a frying pan (including cast-iron pans) after cooking with oil. Remnants of the fat can initiate a harshening process that

continues the next time you use the pan. In India, I learned to boil pans clean with water and potato peels.

- Avoid food oils such as soy oil, corn oil, and sunflower oil (except for high-oleic sunflower oil) because they contain very high levels of omega-6s and few omega-3s.
- For frying at high temperatures, such as stir-frying, choose an oil with a high smoke point, such as clarified butter, canola oil, avocado oil, or peanut oil.
- Add garlic and ginger to stir-fry oil to decrease the development of free radicals and destructive fatty acids in the oil.
- Use oils with a low smoke point, such as extra-virgin olive oil, in vinaigrettes or to drizzle over cooked/fried food. You can bake and fry in olive oil at moderate temperatures (up to 350°F/180°C).
- Use cold-pressed coconut oil (rich in beneficial saturated fats and medium chain triglycerides) at medium temperature because the smoke point for it is 340°F (171°C).
- Store flavorful cold-pressed oils such as avocado oil, flaxseed oil, hazelnut oil, and walnut oil in the refrigerator.

OILS FOR EVERYDAY USE
Olive Oil, Extra-Virgin
Cold-pressed olive oil preserves all the good characteristics of the fruit, such as flavor and aroma. When cold-pressed olive oil is used for sautéing, the flavor changes. A low smoke point means it quickly acquires a burnt flavor. Refined olive oil tolerates a higher heat than cold-pressed and is good for frying.
Fat: Saturated 13 g, monounsaturated 74 g, polyunsaturated 7 g
Use: Salads, dressings, marinades, sauces; can be used for cooking but smokes at low temperatures and then acquires a burnt flavor
Smoke point: Cold-pressed 320°F (160°C)

Canola Oil
Rich in omega-3 fatty acids, neutral flavor, cholesterol reducing, and tolerates high heat and is good for cooking.
Fat: Saturated 7 g, monounsaturated 59 g, polyunsaturated 27 g
Use: Sautéing, stir-fries, salad dressings, mayonnaise
Smoke point: 355°–390°F (180°–200°C)

OILS FOR FLAVOR
Sesame Oil
Nutty flavor.
Fat: Saturated 14 g, monounsaturated 37 g, polyunsaturated 43 g
Use: Stir-fries, other Asian dishes
Smoke point: 400°F (200°C)
Peanut Oil
Peanut flavor.
Fat: Saturated 16 g, monounsaturated 54 g, polyunsaturated 22 g
Use: Dressings, to enhance flavor of vegetables and chicken, stir-fries, deep-frying
Smoke point: 390°F (200°C)

Walnut Oil
Rich in omega-3 fatty acids.
Fat: Saturated 9 g, monounsaturated 22 g, polyunsaturated 63 g
Use: Dressings, to enhance the flavor of cooked vegetables or desserts
Smoke point: 320°F (160°C)

RARER OILS
Wheat Germ Oil
Good source of E vitamins.
Fat: Saturated 18 g, monounsaturated 16 g, polyunsaturated 60 g
Use: As a supplement, enhances other foods as a vitamin source

RECIPE INDEX

> WE CAN THANK EACH OTHER, KJARTAN.

> YES, GREAT TO WORK WITH YOU, BERIT.

ACKNOWLEDGEMENTS

Arne Bru Haug, who took the photos for the book.
Your photos are authentic and down-to-earth. The mood you
created was essential for making the book so fine.
Borghild Fiskå, who helped me write the recipes and text.
You are a perfectionist right down to the pencil tip.
Your help has been indispensable.
Kristoffer Kibart, who always says yes.
You are the best assistant imaginable.
Pavel Pavlov, who is one of the best dessert chefs I know,
uncompromising and inspiring.
Ann Kristin Bjørge, who took such care making sure
the mood in the backgrounds were harmonious.
Thank you to Lars Røtterud, who created this good idea and,
not least, because you introduced me to Berit Nordstrand.
Thank you to the designer, Kristine Lillevik.
Thanks to OBH Nordica for lending us the equipment.
Thanks to Alexander Stensrud for letting us use the cabin.

ARNE BRU HAUG | BORGHILD FISKÅ | KRISTOFFER KIBART | PAVEL PAVLOV | ANN KRISTIN BJØRGE

weldon**owen**

Published in North America by Weldon Owen, Inc.

1045 Sansome Street, Suite 100

San Francisco, CA 94111

www.weldonowen.com

Weldon Owen is a division of Bonnier Publishing USA

Copyright © 2015

© Gyldendal Norsk Forlag AS, Gyldendal Literature

Photos in the book taken by: Arne Bru Haug

Book set with: Festivo and Proxima

Originally published as *Verdens Beste Familie-Kokebok Sunt, Kjapt & Godt*

First published in Norway in 2015 by

Gyldendal Norsk Forlag AS, Gyldendal Literature

English translation by Carol Huebscher Rhoades

Library of Congress Cataloging in Publication data is available.

This edition printed in 2016

10 9 8 7 6 5 4 3 2 1

ISBN 13: 978-1-68188-113-3

ISBN 10: 1-68188-113-6

Printed and bound in Latvia